THE FATHER OF ISRAEL
Trusting God's Promises

JOHN MACARTHUR

THOMAS NELSON
Since 1798

NASHVILLE   DALLAS   MEXICO CITY   RIO DE JANEIRO

Published in Nashville, Tennessee, by Thomas Nelson. Thomas Nelson is a trademark of Thomas Nelson, Inc.

Published in association with the literary agency of Wolgemuth & Associates, Inc.

Layout, design, and writing assistance by Gregory C. Benoit Publishing, Old Mystic, CT ℊᴛB

Thomas Nelson, Inc. titles may be purchased in bulk for educational, business, fund-raising, or sales promotional use. For information, please e-mail *SpecialMarkets@ThomasNelson.com*.

Scripture quotations are taken from THE NEW KING JAMES VERSION. Copyright © 1982 by Thomas Nelson, Inc. Used by permission. All rights reserved.

"Unleashing God's Truth, One Verse at a Time" is a trademark of Grace to You. All rights reserved.

MacArthur Old Testament Study Guide Series, Volume 2

The Father of Israel: Trusting God's Promises

ISBN 978-1-4185-3323-6

Printed in the United States of America

13 14 QG 24 23 22 21

Contents

~ ⌇ ~

CANAAN IN ABRAHAM'S DAY

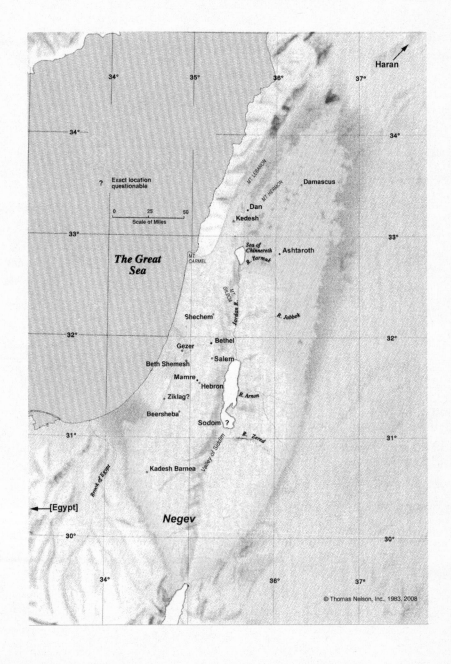

Haran

34°   35°   36°   37°

34°

? Exact location
questionable

MT. LEBANON

MT. HERMON

Damascus

Dan
Kedesh

0   25   50
Scale of Miles

33°

Sea of
Chinnereth

Ashtaroth

**The Great
Sea**

MT.
CARMEL

R. Yarmuk

MT.
GILEAD

Jordan R.

R. Jabbok

Shechem

32°

Bethel

Gezer

Salem

Beth Shemesh

Mamre

Hebron

R. Arnon

Ziklag?

Beersheba

Sodom ?

31°

R. Zered

Valley of Siddim

Kadesh Barnea

Brook of Egypt

← [Egypt]

Negev

30°

34°   36°   37°

INTRODUCTION

The men known as "the patriarchs" (Abraham, Isaac, and Jacob) lived during the Old Testament before Israel's captivity in Egypt. They were the "fathers" of the Jewish people because their descendents became the nation of Israel. These men and their wives were also great saints of the faith, the faith that finds its fulfillment in the person and work of Jesus Christ.

Each was a very real human being, made of the same flesh as you and me and with similar strengths and weaknesses. Each was also called by God to a unique walk of faith, facing unique circumstances and challenges along the way. But their faith is the very thing that unites them: every one of these patriarchs lived a life characterized by faith in God.

In these twelve studies, we will jump back and forth in chronological history, looking at one historical period and then skipping forward or backward in time as needed. We will examine Abram's call to live in Canaan, Sarah's act of faith in God's promise for a son (even at the age of ninety), Jacob's wrestling match with God, and much more. But through it all, we will also learn some precious truths about the character of God, and we will see His great faithfulness in keeping His promises. We will learn, in short, what it means to walk by faith.

∽ What We'll Be Studying ∽

This study guide is divided into four distinct sections in which we will examine selected Bible passages:

Section 1: History. In this first section, we will focus on the historical setting of our Bible text. These five lessons will give a broad overview of the people, places, and events that are important to this study. They will also provide the background for the next two sections. This is our most purely historical segment, focusing simply on what happened and why.

Section 2: Characters. The four lessons in this section will give us an opportunity to zoom in on the characters from our Scripture passages. Some of these people were introduced in section 1, but in this part of the study guide we will take a much closer look at these personalities. Why did God see fit to include them in His Book in the first place?

What made them unique? What can we learn from their lives? In this practical section, we will answer all of these questions and more, as we learn how to live wisely by emulating the wisdom of those who came before us.

Section 3: Themes. Section 3 consists of two lessons in which we will consider some of the broader themes and doctrines touched on in our selected Scripture passages. This is the guide's most abstract portion, wherein we will ponder specific doctrinal and theological questions that are important to the church today. As we ask what these truths mean to us as Christians, we will also look for practical ways to base our lives upon God's truth.

Section 4: Summary. In our final section, we will look back at the principles that we have discovered in the scriptures throughout this study guide. These will be our "take-away" principles, those which permeate the Bible passages that we have studied. As always, we will be looking for ways to make these truths a part of our everyday lives.

⌁ About the Lessons ⌁

⤇ Each study begins with an introduction that provides the background for the selected Scripture passages.

⤇ To assist you in your reading, a section of notes—a miniature Bible commentary of sorts—offers both cultural information and additional insights.

⤇ A series of questions is provided to help you dig a bit deeper into the Bible text.

⤇ Overriding principles brought to light by the Bible text will be studied in each lesson. These principles summarize a variety of doctrines and practical truths found throughout the Bible.

⤇ Finally, additional questions will help you mine the deep riches of God's Word and, most importantly, to apply those truths to your own life.

SECTION 1:

HISTORY

In This Section:

I

LEAVING UR

∽ HISTORICAL BACKGROUND ∾

We will open our studies by meeting a man named Abram. At this point, we know very little about him. What we do know is that he is seventy-five years old, lives with his father in a place called Haran, and has a nephew named Lot. But in the coming studies, we will discover that this man is destined to become the father of the Jewish people and an important link in the family line of Jesus Himself.

The Bible introduces Abram (whose name will be changed to Abraham in the future) by telling us that the Lord had already spoken to him in the past. God told him to leave his father's house and travel "to a land that I will show you" (Genesis 12:1). Evidently, Abram did not know where he would be heading or what he would find when he got there. It is little wonder, in human terms, that he was hesitant to leave his family and homeland—indeed, it is a wonder that he had the faith to obey at all. But this is the major characteristic of the man we know as Abraham: he was a man of *faith*.

In Abram's day, the area we know as the Middle East was already settled to some extent by many different people groups. As yet, though, there was no group of people known as Israelites or Jews; Abram himself would be the first to be called a Hebrew (meaning "one who descended from Eber"). There was also no central authority or domineering nation ruling over the region. There were, however, many fortified cities scattered around the area from Haran in the north down at least to the southerly tip of the Dead Sea, which is probably where Sodom and Gomorrah were located. The people known as the Philistines, who would one day play a major role in David's life, had already begun to settle in the area we know today as the Gaza Strip.

Traveling in this region was not like taking a road trip across the United States, where one drives on highways, eats at McDonald's, and stays at comfortable hotels. It could be a very dangerous business, and one was at risk from bandits and natural hazards. People, therefore, traveled in groups—merchants used large caravans to carry merchandise from place to place—and such processions usually included armed guards to protect against attack. In the southern regions, water and food were not readily available, so a traveling party needed to know where they were going, how they would get there, and what supplies they would need along the way. And God called Abram to start walking—without his extended family, without a destination, and without any guarantee except His own promise.

⌒ READING GENESIS 12 ⌒

GOD'S CALL: *One day the Lord spoke to Abram, probably in a vision or dream, and commanded him to leave his home and family.*

1. THE LORD HAD SAID: It appears that God had called Abram on a previous occasion, telling him to leave his father's house and head south. Apparently, he had obeyed God partway by moving from Ur (whose location is uncertain) to Haran—along with his father's entire household. It is worth noting that we know nothing about him until he began to obey. If Abram had continued to ignore God's call, we would probably never have heard of him—and he would not have become the father of God's chosen nation. It is characteristic of his life, however, that he obeyed God's call, as we see him beginning to do here.

ABRAM: God would change his name to Abraham, but not until after he was circumcised. God did not outline His entire plan for Abram right from the beginning. Instead, He told Abram what the final outcome would be—that he would become a great nation—and then told him what the next step would require. God would reveal His plan for the next step only after Abram obeyed the immediate one.

GET OUT OF YOUR COUNTRY: This would be Abram's first step: he was to leave Haran, where his family lived and where he may have lived for a long time, and head south. But God did *not* tell him where the destination was. The command was simply, "Get out!"

TO A LAND THAT I WILL SHOW YOU: This was actually a very big request for Abram. With the exception of his wife Sarai and his nephew, Lot, Abram was to leave his family and friends behind and head out for a land where he knew nobody and would encounter different cultures and various dangers—without even knowing his final destination. We will discover, however, that this is precisely what God wanted him to experience, because Abram was destined to become a picture of God's people. Abram wandered about without making this world his home, because he had his heart set on an eternal kingdom that God Himself was building. (See Hebrews 11.)

2. I WILL MAKE YOU A GREAT NATION: Abram was destined to become the father of the Israelites. Through him would come Messiah, Jesus the Christ, whose death and

6

resurrection would one day provide salvation for the entire human race. However, Abram was already seventy-five years old when God made this promise—and he had no children! This element of God's promises would prove the most difficult for Abram, and ultimately it would be the greatest test that Abram would face—especially when called upon to sacrifice his only son. But right from the beginning, Abram obeyed God and believed in His promises—even though they seemed ridiculously impossible.

3. IN YOU ALL THE FAMILIES OF THE EARTH SHALL BE BLESSED: God's prophecies of blessing would actually begin to come true within Abram's lifetime, as we will see in future studies. But the greater fulfillment would come when God Himself entered the world through Abram's descendants in the person of Jesus Christ.

ABRAM'S OBEDIENCE: *Abram obeyed God's call, after some apparent delay, and left his home in Haran.*

4. SO ABRAM DEPARTED: As we have seen, it seems to have taken Abram a while to obey God's call to leave Haran, but he eventually did. God demonstrated His patience and grace toward Abram frequently, and Abram demonstrated his own desire to please God by obeying His commands. Nevertheless, Abram was still a real human being, and there were times when he fell far short of perfection.

LOT WENT WITH HIM: Lot was Abram's nephew, and he would cause real problems for Abram in the future—indeed, his presence with Abram would have an impact on the people who lived in Sodom and Gomorrah.

ABRAM WAS SEVENTY-FIVE YEARS OLD: It is true that people lived much longer in Abram's day than we do in modern times, yet seventy-five was still old! It is no small thing to ask a man in his midseventies to pack up and move away from his homeland where he has lived most of his life and from his friends and family. Imagine how difficult it was for Abram to set forth on an exciting adventure at such an advanced age.

5. SARAI HIS WIFE: In the future, God would change her name to Sarah.

LOT HIS BROTHER'S SON: As stated previously, Lot was Abram's nephew. The fact that he accompanied Abram will later become significant.

THE PEOPLE WHOM THEY HAD ACQUIRED IN HARAN: This probably refers to household servants rather than slaves. We will discover that Abram and Lot were very wealthy, and their households were quite large. As we study the life of Abram, it will be important to understand that his entourage included a great many people and large herds of livestock.

SO THEY CAME TO THE LAND OF CANAAN: See the map that follows for background on the geography of the region. The "land of Canaan" indicates that the descendants of Canaan (Ham's son) had settled a large portion of the land that God was planning to give to Abram's descendants. Moses wrote the book of Genesis when the people of Israel—the descendants of Abram—were preparing to enter the promised land. The region was filled with people the Israelites would have to fight to take possession, and many of these people were descended from Ham. See Genesis 9:20–25 for background on these people.

6. SHECHEM: Shechem is about halfway through the land of Canaan in the area known as the Fertile Crescent. See the map on page 11.

THE CANAANITES WERE THEN IN THE LAND: Put yourself in Abram's place: you have been called by God to travel to an undefined location, with the understanding that He is going to give you many descendants and make your family into a great nation. But then you arrive to find that the land is already populated—by people who are likely to be hostile to you! Most people would have balked at this point, wondering whether they had made a mistake. But Abram stepped out in faith, and God faithfully honored that.

7. THEN THE LORD APPEARED TO ABRAM: At this point, God bolstered Abram's faith by reiterating His promise—and by adding some new information to it. In the future, the Lord would appear often to Abram to reiterate His promise and to reveal new details of that promise—but only *after* Abram first obeyed what he'd been told to do. Here, Abram had finally obeyed God's command to travel to Canaan, so God encouraged his faith.

TO YOUR DESCENDANTS I WILL GIVE THIS LAND: This is a new piece of information. Prior to this, God had only told Abram that he would become a great nation, but here God told Abram that his descendants would inherit the entire land of Canaan. God was encouraging Abram to trust Him at His word, despite appearances and circumstances. Even though the land was already settled and populated—with people who were not likely to be friendly to Abram—God insisted that He would one day give the entire land to Abram's descendants. Circumstances made that promise seem impossible, yet Abram continued to place his faith in God's word.

HE BUILT AN ALTAR TO THE LORD: This act demonstrates that Abram chose to believe God, even when His promise seemed impossible. Everywhere Abram traveled, he built altars to the Lord and proclaimed His name to the people around him.

8. HE MOVED FROM THERE: Abram's life would be characterized by his constant moving from one place to another. He was to never settle permanently in any one location, and he would spend the remainder of his days living in tents rather than in a permanent house. (It is very likely that he and his family lived in houses, rather than tents, when they were in Haran.)

CALLED ON THE NAME OF THE LORD: The Hebrew word translated "called" means "to cry out" or "to proclaim." Abram worshiped God in a very public manner, proclaiming His character to the people around him. Remember that there were many people traveling with Abram as part of his household, as well as those traveling in Lot's household. In proclaiming God publicly, Abram was already beginning to fulfill his role as a blessing to the nations.

FAMINE: *Abram had been wandering about in the land of Canaan, living in a tent and pasturing his flocks. Then along came trouble . . .*

---

10. THERE WAS A FAMINE IN THE LAND: Famine and the land of Egypt figured prominently in the history of Israel, right up to their exodus from Egypt. God uses the circumstances of our lives—both good things and bad, blessings and trials—to lead us in His will. This particular famine would lead Abram to a time of testing in Egypt, just as it would someday lead to a time of blessing in Egypt for Abram's descendants. (See Genesis 47:27.)

FEAR: *Abram began to fear what would happen to him in Egypt, and he talked himself into fearing the worst. This lack of trust had long-term consequences for him, his family, and the world as a whole.*

---

11. YOU ARE A WOMAN OF BEAUTIFUL COUNTENANCE: Sarai was sixty-five when Abram (aged seventy-five) left Haran. It is unclear how much time had passed, but she was at least in her late sixties.

12. IT WILL HAPPEN: Here we see Abram struggling with a lack of faith in God's promises. He had convinced himself in fear that bad things were going to happen, yet they never did. Fear leads God's people into doubt, not faith, and the Lord Himself commands us frequently in the Bible to "be of good courage" and "fear not."

THEY WILL KILL ME: Abram was made of the same flesh that we are, which is encouraging news. Here he lapsed from his great faith in God's promises. If he had clung to His promises, he would have realized that the Egyptians *couldn't* kill him, because he already knew he was destined to become a great nation—but he didn't have any children yet. Therefore his own logic could have reassured him that he had to live at least long enough to have offspring. But fear had blinded both logic and faith.

13. SAY [THAT] YOU ARE MY SISTER: This was partially true, for Sarai was actually Abram's half sister; they shared the same father but different mothers. Nevertheless, a half truth is still a lie, and it got Abram and his wife into trouble—more than once! What is worse, he was encouraging his wife—and probably the rest of his household—to sin.

15. THE WOMAN WAS TAKEN TO PHARAOH'S HOUSE: This statement is loaded with significance because it implies that Abram did nothing to prevent it. Abram had effectively allowed another man to take his wife, with the intentions of making her part of his harem. Fear had driven Abram so far from being a man of faith that he sold out his own wife.

16. HE TREATED ABRAM WELL FOR HER SAKE: And now we discover that Abram was even making a *profit* from the situation, like a pimp with his prostitute. This is a low point in Abram's walk with God.

MALE AND FEMALE SERVANTS: Pharaoh gave Abram many gifts, including "male and female servants." It is quite possible that Hagar was one of these female servants, and she would bring further trouble to Abram in the future.

GOD INTERVENES: *Abram's lack of faith actually endangered the very plan of God for the coming Messiah. But God will not permit man's actions to interfere with His plans.*

17. THE LORD PLAGUED PHARAOH AND HIS HOUSE WITH GREAT PLAGUES BECAUSE OF SARAI: The significance of Abram's action is much deeper than lying about his wife: he was actually putting God's promise of a Messiah at risk. After all, God intended to bring His Redeemer through Abram's seed. God would later make it very clear that He meant to bring about His chosen people (and His Chosen One) through the offspring of Abram and Sarai (Abraham and Sarah). Yet here was Abram, offering his wife to another man, with the very real possibility that Sarai would have that man's child. For this reason, and because Sarai was the one in real peril from a human perspective, God intervened to protect her from becoming one of Pharaoh's wives.

18. WHAT IS THIS [THAT] YOU HAVE DONE TO ME?: Abram's lack of faith also placed Pharaoh and his entire household in jeopardy. This is a principle of sin, that one man's sin will often endanger many others. What's worse, Pharaoh had not done anything to threaten Abram; indeed, he had been generous in giving him gifts. The whole problem arose because Abram became afraid and failed to place his trust in God's protection. Alas, this entire sad episode would be repeated when Abraham met Abimelech, another king. (See Genesis 20.)

THE JOURNEYS OF ABRAM

⌁ FIRST IMPRESSIONS ⌁

1. If you had been in Abram's place, how would you have responded to God's command to leave your home and family?

2. What were the costs to Abram to obey God's call?

3. *When have you been called to make a radical change in your own life for God? What were the costs? The results?*

4. *Why did Abram lie to Pharaoh? How do you think it made Sarai feel? How might you have responded if you were in Pharaoh's place?*

↶ Some Key Principles ↷

God calls His people to walk in faith.

God revealed a small portion of His plan to Abram, and then He asked Abram to respond by walking away from all that he knew as home and family. In fact, He asked Abram to walk into a strange land without even knowing exactly where he was going or what he would find when he got there.

This is what it means to walk in faith: to step into the unknown, even into threatening circumstances, with only God's word to depend on. Abram arrived in Canaan to find himself surrounded with unfriendly people, and God then told him that he would inherit the entire land for his descendants. Circumstances made this seem impossible, yet Abram believed God and took Him at His word. He was seventy-five years old and had no children, yet he believed that God was going to give him many descendants.

Walking in faith requires that we accept God's Word at face value, even when it seems impossible that His promises can come true. In this, Abram and Sarai provide us a great role model.

Often God will not reveal the next step until we obey the present step.

Abram understood only that he would have children and that those children would become a great nation. He did not know where they would live or how such things could be accomplished—all he knew was that God wanted him to leave Haran and move to Canaan. It was not until he arrived in Canaan that God told him the next part of His plan: to give his descendants the entire land of Canaan as their home.

The truth is that God's plan for Abram's descendants went way beyond acquiring the promised land and becoming a great nation. Ultimately, God was planning to bring forth His Messiah, His Son Jesus, through the descendants of Abram. He did not know any of these details, yet God expected him to obey just the same.

God expects His children today to live the same way. He does not always reveal to us the fullness of His plans for our lives and the lives of those we influence. Instead, He tells us what we need to know in order to obey Him one step at a time. To discover the next step in His plan, we must first obey the present step.

Fear is the enemy of God's people.

Fear is what led Abram to make a disastrous blunder in Egypt. Fear would lead him to make the same *exact* mistake later. He became afraid of the unknown in Egypt, even after he had trusted God with the great unknown of Canaan. Had he reminded himself of God's faithfulness in Canaan and of God's promise that he would become a great nation, Abram might have conquered his fear and continued to live by faith.

Satan loves to use fear to draw God's people out of obedience. When this happens, they are tempted to take matters into their own hands. Abram took matters into his own hands, devising what he thought was a clever plan to avoid being killed, and the results were very bad and far-reaching. Today, the evil one uses fear—of the future, the past, and the present—to mislead us in the same way, so that our choices, too, reap results that are negative and far-reaching. When anxiety creeps in, we are wise to remind ourselves of all that God has done for us already and to focus our minds on His promises. God's Word drives out the devil's fears.

∽ Digging Deeper ∾

5. *Why did God call Abram to leave Haran in the first place? To leave his father's household? Why couldn't he just stay where he was?*

6. Why does God often only reveal His will one step at a time? Why does He not give us a clear outline of all that He has planned?

7. In what ways did God lead Abram in this chapter? How does He lead His people today?

8. How does Satan use fear today to lead people away from God?

➻ Taking It Personally ➻

9. What step of obedience is God asking of you today? What is it going to cost you?

10. What fears are you facing? What circumstances or "unknowns" are taking your eyes off of trusting God? What scriptures can help you place your trust back in God's faithfulness?

2

THE PROMISE TO ABRAM

GENESIS 13, 15

➷ HISTORICAL BACKGROUND ⤻

Abram was living in Canaan, moving from place to place, dwelling in tents. From a human perspective, there was no reason for him to not settle in one location, build permanent structures, and even fortify the area with a large wall—even establish a small standing army. Had he done that, Abram would have been just like his neighbors. Those neighbors might have been uncomfortable to have a man of such great wealth establish yet another stronghold in their region, but in time everyone might have adjusted.

This was the age of great empires, such as Egypt, which flourished with majestic architecture, art, and politics. Even smaller city-states were fortified with surrounding walls, heavy gates, and well-trained armies.

Much of Canaan consisted of the area known as the Fertile Crescent, an arc of land today that is well watered and productive. If you look at the map on page 11, the arrows showing Abraham's journeys roughly define the Fertile Crescent, arcing from Ur down to Beersheba. The area south of Beersheba, called the Negev, is much more arid and rocky. This region is suitable for grazing flocks in the summer season, but shepherds must move their flocks north for pasture during other times of the year.

This lifestyle is the one Abram chose, rather than settling himself inside of solid city walls. He spent the remainder of his life as a nomad, moving from place to place and pasturing his flocks where there was food, as dictated by the seasons. This is not normal behavior for a man of great wealth and power (he actually defeated the armies of four kings—see Genesis 14). In order to understand his motives, we must look more closely at the promise from God—for it was on this promise that Abram was making his decisions and building for his future.

⌃ READING GENESIS 13:14–18 ⌃

PROMISE OF LAND: *Abram first had to part company with his nephew Lot. Once that happened, God would reveal more of His promise.*

14. AFTER LOT HAD SEPARATED FROM HIM: Due to the fact that their flocks were competing, Abram and Lot decided to separate. (See Genesis 13:5–13.) Once Lot had gone, the Lord was ready to appear to Abram with further information concerning His promise.

THE PLACE WHERE YOU ARE: Abram was encamped near Bethel, which is roughly at the center of the area that would come to be known as Palestine.

15. ALL THE LAND: The land of Canaan. Moses wrote the book of Genesis during the time when the Israelites were wandering in the wilderness, and perhaps just prior to the time when they would enter the land of Canaan and claim it as their own. But the Israelites had already surveyed the promised land and discovered that the people who dwelled in the land were "strong" and their cities were "fortified and very large" (Numbers 13:28).

I GIVE TO YOU AND YOUR DESCENDANTS FOREVER: It was important for the Israelites to understand *why* they were claiming the promised land, because they had lost heart on the verge of entering it. Moses reminded them in this passage that God had promised Canaan to Abram's descendants, and they could therefore trust Him to protect them as they entered it.

PROMISE OF DESCENDANTS: *God had already promised Abram that he would have children, but here He revealed that Abram's descendants would be innumerable.*

16. I WILL MAKE YOUR DESCENDANTS AS THE DUST OF THE EARTH: This promise was fulfilled literally in the physical descendants of Abram. In Solomon's day, "Judah and Israel were as numerous as the sand by the sea in multitude" (1 Kings 4:20). Yet it is also fulfilled to an even greater extent when we add in the countless multitudes who have accepted Christ and, spiritually speaking, become "the seed of Abraham." Galatians 3:29 says, "And if you are Christ's, then you are Abraham's seed, and heirs according to the promise."

18. ABRAM MOVED HIS TENT: This, as we have seen, was the pattern for the remainder of Abram's life: he never stayed in one place for an extended length of time. Genesis reminds us of his unsettled life repeatedly, and the New Testament tells us that Abraham is an example for God's people to follow. We are called to be "strangers and pilgrims on the earth" (Hebrews 11:13), always focusing our eyes upon eternity.

BUILT AN ALTAR THERE TO THE LORD: This, too, was a pattern in Abram's life: wherever he went, he built an altar and called upon the name of the Lord. Building an altar in Abram's culture was a very public statement of what god a person worshiped. Abram's household consisted of a great many people; when he built an altar and offered a sacrifice, he was leading many hundreds of people—perhaps more than a thousand—in worshiping the Lord.

⌒ READING GENESIS 15:1–21 ⌒

GOD PROMISES HIMSELF: *Next God would reveal to Abram the greatest detail of all His promises: He Himself would be Abram's "exceedingly great reward" (Genesis 15:1).*

1. DO NOT BE AFRAID, ABRAM: We will soon discover that Abram was afraid that God's promises could not come true—at least, not without Abram's help. We already saw this in the passages from Study 1; we will see it carried even further when Abram attempts to sire a son through his wife's maid, Hagar. Fear leads people to move away from faith rather than toward it.

I AM YOUR . . . EXCEEDINGLY GREAT REWARD: This is actually the very core of God's promises to Abram and to his descendants—God was promising Himself, not merely many descendants and a nice piece of real estate. Abram's descendants would be the ones to bring forth the Messiah, God's only Son, and through Him the entire human race would regain access into the presence of God.

ABRAM NEEDS REASSURANCE: *Despite all of God's personal appearances to Abram, he was still unsure that the promises would come to pass. Why? Because Abram was a man, just like us.*

2. WHAT WILL YOU GIVE ME: This is a rather bold question for a sinful man to pose to the almighty God, as if demanding some proof that He would keep His word. God had already visited Abram several times, reiterating His promise of an heir and a home. Abram had done nothing to deserve this promise—God did not owe him anything. Nevertheless, God here demonstrated His great mercy and patience by honoring Abram's request.

3. You have given me no offspring: It had been years since God first appeared to him and promised him descendants—and yet no son had been born. We need to remember that Abram was only a man, and even a man of great faith will need some encouragement from time to time if he is to hold firm to trusting God's word.

4. This one shall not be your heir: That is, the man named Eliezer of Damascus. (See Genesis 15:2.)

one who will come from your own body shall be your heir: Abram would later take this promise in the narrowest interpretation, allowing his wife to persuade him to have a child with one of his servants. God would make it more abundantly clear to Abram in the future that his heir would come not only from his own body but from his wife's own body too. The difficulty for Abram was that he was at least eighty years old by this time, and his wife at least seventy. God was asking Abram to place his faith in something that was completely impossible.

Abram's Righteousness: *Abram believed God's word—even before He had sealed the covenant in ritual fashion—and God counted this as righteousness.*

---

6. he believed in the Lord: We will consider this important verse in more detail in Study 6, but for now it is important to recognize that this was at the core of Abram's character: he believed God. Even though God was asking him to believe in something that was utterly impossible; even though his own eyes told him that the promise hadn't come true for years already; even though he had no guarantee to bank on other than God's word—Abram believed in the Lord.

He accounted it to him for righteousness: Abram (later called Abraham) is the "father of our faith," and we as Christians are called "sons of Abraham." The reason for this high honor is that Abram demonstrated the basic ingredient of being reconciled with God: faith. The New Testament uses Abram as the type of those who are saved by faith in Jesus Christ. "Now it was not written for [Abram's] sake alone that it was imputed to him, but also for us. It shall be imputed to us who believe in Him who raised up Jesus our Lord from the dead, who was delivered up because of our offenses, and was raised because of our justification" (Romans 4:23–25).

The Covenant: *God next had Abram set out his culture's equivalent of a legal contract. By performing this ritual, God bound Himself to fulfill His promise.*

---

9. a three-year-old heifer: God made a covenant with Abram. This was an unconditional covenant, which means that God committed Himself to fulfill the covenant regardless of what Abram did; no commitment was required of Abram for the covenant to be valid. (God did make such conditional covenants in other passages.) The animals that God commanded Abram to sacrifice in this covenant were the very same animals included in the entire law that He would later reveal to Moses. The laws of sacrifices were complex and demanding, but the one thing that was consistent throughout the entire law is this: without the shedding of blood, there can be no remission of sins. (See Hebrews 9:22.)

10. CUT THEM IN TWO: Ancient covenants often involved this form of animal sacrifice. An animal was cut in half, and the two parties to the covenant walked between them. This was a symbolic way of saying, "May the same happen to me if I do not keep this covenant." (See Jeremiah 34:18–19.)

12. A DEEP SLEEP FELL UPON ABRAM: We are not specifically told how God appeared to Abram in each instance, but it appears that He only came to him in dreams or visions up to this point. God did appear in person before Abraham later, but only after he was circumcised.

HORROR AND GREAT DARKNESS FELL UPON HIM: This in part signified to Abram the period of slavery that his descendants would endure in Egypt prior to the Exodus.

PROPHECIES OF THE FUTURE: *God now revealed to Abram some of His plan for the future of his descendants. These prophecies foretold Israel's captivity and escape from Egypt.*

13. YOUR DESCENDANTS WILL BE STRANGERS: The Israelites would eventually become slaves in Egypt after Joseph's reign. They were destined to serve in slavery for 430 years before God brought them out under the leadership of Moses. Remember that Moses himself was writing Genesis during that very exodus, and these historical passages undoubtedly helped the Israelites find encouragement during their wanderings in the wilderness.

14. THE NATION WHOM THEY SERVE I WILL JUDGE: God would send plagues upon Egypt to force Pharaoh to release the Israelites, and He would finally destroy the Egyptian army when it pursued His people into the wilderness.

THEY SHALL COME OUT WITH GREAT POSSESSIONS: God directed the Israelites to "spoil the Egyptians" before leaving. (See Exodus 11:2.)

15. A GOOD OLD AGE: Abraham lived to be 175. (See Genesis 25:7.)

16. THE INIQUITY OF THE AMORITES IS NOT YET COMPLETE: God demonstrated His mercy and patience repeatedly in the book of Genesis, offering men many opportunities to repent and find salvation. But the time did come when a man's—and a nation's—

stubborn wickedness reached its full measure. At that point, the justice of God fell. Once the iniquity of the Amorites reached its full measure, God would send His people into the land to eradicate them.

17. A SMOKING OVEN AND A BURNING TORCH: These items symbolized the presence of God, who solemnly promised by divine oath to fulfill His word to Abram. Old Testament manifestations of God's presence frequently emphasize His justice and power. In this case, the oven and torch may suggest God's burning zeal and His potential wrath.

PASSED BETWEEN THOSE PIECES: It is interesting to notice that Abram never passed between the sacrificed animals—only God passed through. This is because Abram had no part in the fulfillment of this covenant—God would make good on His promises to Abram regardless of the future actions of Abram and his descendants.

⌇ FIRST IMPRESSIONS ⌇

1. Why do you think God reiterated His promise to Abram after he and Lot parted company? Look at Genesis 13:5–13. How would you have responded to Lot if you had been in Abram's position?

2. If you had been Abram, knowing that you and your wife were both growing old, how would you have viewed God's promise that you would have a son?

3. How would you have viewed His promise concerning inheriting land? Would you have continued living as a nomad or done something different?

4. How does knowing the end of Abram's story change the way you view the doubts and fears that Abram faced? What should that teach us about the doubts and fears that we face?

～ Some Key Principles ～

God's plans are bigger than we can understand.

God revealed His plans to Abram concerning a son and a promised land, and these promises were immensely important to Abram. Yet they were actually just a very small part of God's larger plan, which was to bring a Redeemer to mankind to release us from sin and death.

Abram could not have understood this larger plan, yet his choice to obey or disobey would have profound ramifications. We saw this in Study 1 when Abram jeopardized God's plan by giving his wife to another man. In this present study, we see how Abram's obedience furthered God's larger plan, eventually leading to our own salvation through Christ.

The principle here is that we must obey what God has called us to do, even though we may not see the bigger picture. God's plans extend beyond our own lives and beyond human history into eternity. Our part is simply to "trust and obey."

God works all things together for good to those who trust Him.

This principle is closely related to the previous one, in that we are called to trust and obey. But the good news is that God's long-term plans for the human race do not override His short-term plans for us as individuals.

God's promises to Abram focused more on his descendants than on him personally. The land of Canaan was promised to his offspring, and he personally never received any place that he could call home. But at the same time, Abram was given something far greater than any piece of real estate: he was granted a personal relationship with God Himself.

The Lord does use His people to further His purposes in the lives of others, but He also pours out blessings upon those people as He uses them. We will see this as we study Abram further in future studies as God draws him into an intimate relationship with Himself and uses him in powerful ways in the land of Canaan. The greatest blessing of all is free to God's people today, just as it was for Abram: an intimate communion with the Creator of all things.

God's people are pilgrims and strangers on earth.

God had promised that Abram's descendants would inherit the land of Canaan, yet Abram himself lived out his days in a tent, roaming from one place to another. Hebrews 11 tells us that he did this because his eyes were focused, not on the land around him—even though it was going to become his—but on the eternal kingdom that God was preparing for His people.

This is to be the attitude of God's people today as well. We must remember that this world is not our home; we are only here temporarily. The world is constantly pressuring us to put down roots, to embrace the culture around us as though we were destined to dwell here forever. But God's people must resist this attitude because no man will remain on earth longer than the span of a human life.

When we accept Jesus as our Lord and Savior, we are born anew into the family of God, and we gain a new inheritance: God's Son Himself. We become heirs of the eternal kingdom of God, and nothing on this planet can compare with what awaits us in eternity. We must keep our eyes always focused on eternity and not allow the things of this world to interfere with our heavenly calling.

ᔕ DIGGING DEEPER ᔓ

5. *What does it mean that God "accounted it to him for righteousness" (Genesis 15:6)?*

6. *Notice that Abram "believed God" even before God sealed His covenant with the sacrificial ritual. Why did he believe God? On what did he base his faith?*

7. *Why did God call Abram to live in tents, even though He intended to give the land to his descendants anyway? Why did He not allow Abram to get settled into Canaan?*

8. Why did God select Abram in the first place? Do you think it was something in Abram or something in God's gracious character that caused God to bring the Messiah through Abram's family line?

∽ TAKING IT PERSONALLY ∽

9. God performed the sacrificial ritual to permanently seal His covenant with Abram. What has He done to seal His promises to you (beginning with the death of His Son on the cross)? What has He promised you?

10. What things are most important to you in your own life? In what ways are you living as a pilgrim on earth? In what ways are you being distracted by the things of this world?

3
DEALING WITH LOT

⌁ HISTORICAL BACKGROUND ⌁

Let's return to the time when Abram was in Egypt, which we looked at briefly in Study 1. This study opens with Abram and his household leaving Egypt. Lot was still with him.

Our passages open with Abram and Lot standing on a high mountainous area, looking out over all of Canaan. Below them to the east was one of the few truly level areas in Canaan, a very fertile valley that is watered by the Jordan River. Not far to the south, at the mouth of that valley, lies what we call today the Dead Sea or the Salt Sea. When Abram and Lot looked out upon that sea, however, it looked very different than it does today— if it existed at all. Where the southern end of the Dead Sea lies today, Abram and Lot looked upon several thriving and prosperous cities: including Sodom and Gomorrah.

Lot would now separate from Abram, and evidently he would continue to live as a nomad for a time. As he traveled, however, he moved closer and closer to the city of Sodom, eventually giving up his nomadic ways and settling into a comfortable urban lifestyle. When we meet him again, he will be sitting in the seat of a city elder, acting as a significant leader in Sodom. Lot will have walked, stood, and finally sat down with the wicked.

⌁ READING GENESIS 13:1–13 ⌁

LEAVING EGYPT: *We open with the time that Abram spent in Egypt, which we looked at in Study 1. We find him heading north into Canaan, finally stopping at Bethel.*

1. ABRAM WENT UP FROM EGYPT: Abram had been staying in Egypt, and during this time he told Pharaoh that his wife was only his sister. See Study 1 and Genesis 12 for more information.

AND LOT WITH HIM: Abram's nephew Lot traveled with Abram, as he had done since the pair left Haran.

TO THE SOUTH: Abram and company were not traveling southward; they were actually heading northeast toward Canaan. But they were entering the southern section of Canaan, known as the Negev. The sense here is that they traveled to the southern sections of Canaan.

2. ABRAM WAS VERY RICH: He also had a great many people traveling with him in his household, as we will see. Lot also evidently had similar wealth.

3. BETHEL: Bethel is located in the hills overlooking the fertile Jordan River valley. That valley was the most level and fertile area in Canaan. See the map in the Introduction.

4. ABRAM CALLED ON THE NAME OF THE LORD: Once again, we see this man of God depending on God in his daily life. This was the pattern wherever Abram went.

TOO MUCH STUFF: *Abram and Lot had grown very wealthy, and the land could not support them both. This wealth would prove to be a trap for Lot.*

5. LOT . . . HAD FLOCKS AND HERDS AND TENTS: Like Abram, Lot probably had numerous servants and hired hands. Each of these people likely had a family, tent, and household possessions, and many probably had livestock of their own.

6. THE LAND WAS NOT ABLE TO SUPPORT THEM: A conservative estimate of Abram's traveling household would be at least one thousand people. He also had flocks of sheep and herds of cattle, and the people who worked for him almost certainly had possessions of their own. Add to this the household of Lot, and we realize that Abram had a very large group of people moving about with him. It would have been difficult to navigate such a large group, and finding suitable grazing and living space would have been a logistical nightmare.

THEIR POSSESSIONS WERE SO GREAT THAT THEY COULD NOT DWELL TOGETHER: Due to the extent of their wealth, it was no longer logistically possible for them to continue traveling together. Here is a tragic fact of our world, that even close kin are driven apart by possessions. We are told, however, that Abram's focus was on the things of eternity rather than the things of this temporal world. Lot, on the other hand, was more interested in temporal gain. His selfish choices would eventually lead him to Sodom and consequently into great spiritual peril.

7. THE CANAANITES AND THE PERIZZITES THEN DWELT IN THE LAND: This is an odd statement to follow the fact that Abram's herdsmen were fighting with Lot's herdsmen. The implication, however, is that the world around Abram was watching, and his strife with Lot was producing a poor testimony.

PARTING COMPANY AT LAST: *After years of traveling together, Abram and Lot finally parted company—each taking a very different path from this point onward. Abram's path would be marked by divine protection, while Lot's path would be characterized by temptation and compromise.*

9. PLEASE SEPARATE FROM ME: After having dwelt together for so long, Abram separated from Lot more by compulsion than by choice. Yet God was using these circumstances to providentially separate Lot from Abram—and to send Abram in the opposite direction from the evil influences of Sodom and Gomorrah.

IF YOU TAKE THE LEFT, THEN I WILL GO TO THE RIGHT: Abram here demonstrated great humility and generosity. By every standard, he had the perfect right to choose for himself first: he was older, he was Lot's uncle, he was head of the household, and so forth. Yet he deferred to his nephew and allowed him to choose where to settle.

10. LOT LIFTED HIS EYES: This interesting phrase appears frequently in Genesis, and it is worthwhile to take note of what each person saw when he lifted his eyes. It will give insight into what was in that person's heart. In this case, Lot lifted his eyes and saw what he most wanted: choice land and wealth.

THE PLAIN OF JORDAN: This is the flat valley where the Jordan River flows, running between the Dead Sea (or Salt Sea) and the Sea of Galilee. This land is very fertile and flat, two important qualities in the land of Canaan. This would have been equivalent to the choicest and most expensive real estate in the entire region. Lot's eye fell on the area where the wealthy dwelled.

BEFORE THE LORD DESTROYED SODOM AND GOMORRAH: It is quite possible that the Dead Sea did not exist or was substantially smaller at this point in history. Sodom probably stood at the south end of what is now the Dead Sea.

LOT'S CHOICE: *Lot looked out on the fertile Jordan River valley below him, and wealth and comfort beckoned to him. He would follow this desire all the way to Sodom.*

11. LOT CHOSE FOR HIMSELF: Abram had just shown great deference toward Lot, and the proper response would have been for Lot to return it back to his uncle, insisting that Abram choose first—as was his right. Instead, Lot chose for himself, looking out for his own interests and satisfying his own desires.

12. ABRAM DWELT IN THE LAND OF CANAAN: In tents, as we have noted previously. This was in stark contrast to the future urban lifestyle of his nephew.

LOT DWELT IN THE CITIES OF THE PLAIN: The cities of Canaan (and beyond) represented a constant threat in the life of Abram. Whenever he went to the city, trouble followed. This pattern also held true for his nephew Lot. The cities of the plain were probably fortified with large walls and standing armies. They were without doubt very wealthy and comfortable, but they were also characterized by great wickedness.

PITCHED HIS TENT EVEN AS FAR AS SODOM: This is probably a figure of speech in this instance, since we discover Lot living in a house inside the walls of Sodom. It is possible, however, that he remained a nomad for a time after leaving Abram, gradually moving south until he came to Sodom, where he settled permanently—or so he thought. The allure of worldly pleasures and comfort frequently work this way, moving us a little at a time, until one day we find ourselves entrenched in the world's system.

13. THE MEN OF SODOM WERE EXCEEDINGLY WICKED: Lot would have known that the people of Sodom were wicked before he even moved into that city. Lot himself was a righteous man, as the New Testament testifies (see 2 Peter 2:7), and one would think he would have been unwilling to live in a city that was renowned for its wickedness. Yet this only serves to demonstrate the deadly power that wealth and comfort can exert on us—even on those who belong to the family of God.

⤳ Reading Genesis 19 ⤳

YEARS LATER: *We now fast-forward a number of years and find that Lot has given up his nomadic lifestyle in favor of settling down in a fortified city. His choice of retirement homes wasn't too good.*

1. LOT WAS SITTING IN THE GATE: This was a sign of respect and authority in the ancient world. The city was probably surrounded by a high wall, and the only way in and out was through a fortified gate. The elders of the city would sit in the gateway and "hold court," acting as judges for the people of the city as well as leaders and decision makers. Lot had risen to prominence in Sodom.

3. ENTERED HIS HOUSE: Lot was no longer living in a tent, but had settled himself comfortably in the city of Sodom. The Bible is clear that "blessed is the man who walks not in the counsel of the ungodly, nor stands in the path of sinners, nor sits in the seat of the scornful" (Psalm 1:1). Lot had, unfortunately, made this very progression by walking as a nomad toward the worldly city of Sodom, then standing together with its residents, and finally sitting in the seat of an elder of that city.

4. ALL THE PEOPLE FROM EVERY QUARTER: Before the angels even had a chance to retire for the night, word spread throughout the city that strangers had come to town— and virtually every male of the city flocked to satisfy his lusts. The picture here is of men who are driven by their lusts, choosing to obey their insatiable and enslaving drives.

SURROUNDED THE HOUSE: These lustful savages had no intention of parley or even seduction; they arrived at Lot's house intent upon violently taking what they wanted.

5. BRING THEM OUT TO US THAT WE MAY KNOW THEM CARNALLY: These men intended to sexually assault the angels, to forcibly indulge in homosexual carnality. Such activity, even today, is known as *sodomy*—whether done voluntarily or otherwise. God condemns every kind of homosexuality. (See Leviticus 20:13 and 1 Corinthians 6:9.)

LOT'S FOLLY: *We now begin to see how Lot's years of following the world's priorities had turned him into a fearful and unwise old man.*

7. PLEASE, MY BRETHREN . . .: Lot had lost his wisdom by living with the wicked men of the world. He demonstrated this when he tried to compromise and hold "peace talks" with these men. But these wicked people were not interested in reason, truth, or compromise, only in satisfying their own desires. Eve made the same mistake when she attempted to debate theology with the devil. (See Genesis 3.) It is telling that Lot referred to these ungodly men as "my brethren." The world is not a brotherhood to God's people.

8. TWO DAUGHTERS WHO HAVE NOT KNOWN A MAN: In a shockingly misguided and unthinkable attempt to protect his angelic guests, Lot suggested that the angry mob be given his two virgin daughters.

YOU MAY DO TO THEM AS YOU WISH: What a tragic picture this presents of how far a man can sink. Lot offered his daughters to be terribly abused and probably killed by an angry mob—an entire city of men. It is tempting to see Lot as a vile man, and in this instance his actions were clearly inexcusable, yet the New Testament refers to him as "righteous Lot" (2 Peter 2:7). This is yet another demonstration of God's grace, able to save even the lowest of sinners.

THEY HAVE COME UNDER THE SHADOW OF MY ROOF: Ancient custom required that a man ensure the safety and comfort of guests within his house. Lot would have been deeply disgraced if the angels had come to harm while in his home. It is sad, however, that he cared more about such social customs than about protecting his daughters—who also lived under his roof.

9. HE KEEPS ACTING AS A JUDGE: These men had willingly submitted to Lot as a judge just a few hours before when he was sitting in the city gate. But this is the way of the world: when a person stands up and tells people not to be unrighteous, they turn around and accuse him of being judgmental.

10. THE MEN REACHED OUT THEIR HANDS: The angels of the Lord did not waste their time and effort trying to reason and plead with the Sodomites. This demonstrates two things: (1) the correct way to deal with the arguments of the world, which is to resist firmly without engaging in empty debate; and (2) the immense grace and mercy of God. Lot was in this mess because of his own poor decisions, yet God came all the way to his house just to rescue him from the coming judgment.

II. BLINDNESS: The men of Sodom were already spiritually blind, and God made them physically blind as well.

GET OUT OF TOWN: *The next morning, Lot was given strict instructions to leave town and not look back. God was extending His mercy specifically to Lot, but Lot still had to obey God's commands.*

---

12. TAKE THEM OUT OF THIS PLACE: Lot's family should not have been in Sodom in the first place.

14. TO HIS SONS-IN-LAW HE SEEMED TO BE JOKING: Lot had apparently not indulged in the sins of Sodom, yet he had still lost his credibility among his neighbors and even his own family. This is an important principle to understand: when we live at peace with the world around us, we risk losing our testimony even if we do not indulge in worldly practices.

16. WHILE HE LINGERED: Lot was having grave difficulty leaving behind all his possessions and comfortable lifestyle. "For where your treasure is, there your heart will be also" (Matthew 6:21).

17. DO NOT LOOK BEHIND YOU: Looking back implies having second thoughts, regrets at what you have left behind in following God's commands. "No one, having put his hand to the plow, and looking back, is fit for the kingdom of God" (Luke 9:62).

ESCAPE TO THE MOUNTAINS: Lot's uncle Abraham was living in the mountains a short way to the northwest. (The angels had covered the distance in less than a day.) If Lot had immediately obeyed what the angels commanded, his final end might have been less disgraceful.

A WEE LITTLE TOWN: *Lot began to let fear take control of his heart, and as a result he forgot to place his faith in the Lord—even after his miraculous rescue.*

---

18. PLEASE, NO, MY LORDS!: It is hard to believe that Lot had the audacity to argue with the Lord's command after all he had been through this day, but it speaks of his long habit of self-indulgence. There is a whining quality to his words here.

LEST SOME EVIL OVERTAKE ME AND I DIE: Lot presented a strong contrast to his uncle Abraham. He had just seen the dramatic rescue and patient grace of God in his life, but here he invented fears of what might happen if he obeyed God's further commands. Abraham, by contrast, obeyed in faith, and it was counted to him as righteousness.

20. PLEASE LET ME ESCAPE THERE (IS IT NOT A LITTLE ONE?): Again we detect a whining, wheedling tone of voice in Lot's words. He was like a spoiled child, intent upon having his own way. In this, he resembled the men of Sodom.

AND MY SOUL SHALL LIVE: Once again, we see that Lot had lost his trust in God's faithfulness. God had gone to great lengths to rescue Lot out of Sodom, "the LORD being merciful to him" (Genesis 19:16), yet his underlying attitude was that God was leading him into some kind of trap. *If I do exactly what the Lord commanded*, he thought, *I will be led into death and my soul shall perish.* This mind-set grows as we become comfortable in the world around us because we begin to think that we have full control over our environment and our destiny. The one who lives by faith, on the other hand, is constantly reminded that he can do nothing without God's help.

JUDGMENT RAINS DOWN: *As soon as Lot and his family were safely out of range, a dreadful cataclysm fell from the sky, destroying both Sodom and Gomorrah.*

21. I WILL NOT OVERTHROW THIS CITY FOR WHICH YOU HAVE SPOKEN: Abraham had pleaded with God the day before to save Sodom and Gomorrah from destruction (see Genesis 18), and here we discover that it was actually God's desire to spare men from judgment. While Abraham begged for mercy for others, Lot was most concerned with his own safety. This is yet another result of making oneself comfortable in the world's system.

25. AND WHAT GREW ON THE GROUND: The area at the southern end of the Dead Sea is characterized by salt and blasted rock. It is not conducive to supporting natural life.

26. HIS WIFE LOOKED BACK: The angels had specifically warned Lot to not look back as they were fleeing. See note on verse 17.

LOT'S SHAMEFUL END: *Lot's fear became his motivating force toward the end of his days, and he once again lost his trust in the Lord. This sad story is the last we hear of him in the Old Testament.*

30. HE WAS AFRAID TO DWELL IN ZOAR: This may be because Lot felt the people in Zoar would blame him for the nearby devastation or because Lot himself was afraid that further destruction might come to the surrounding areas. In either case, we again see Lot motivated by fear rather than by faith. This is in direct contrast to the confidence in God that characterized his uncle Abraham.

31. THERE IS NO MAN ON THE EARTH TO COME IN TO US: Now we find that Lot's daughters suffered from fear just as their father did. They persuaded themselves that there was "no man on the earth" for them to marry—a rather absurd conclusion, as though the destruction of Sodom and Gomorrah had destroyed the entire earth and all its inhabitants. Once again, we see how fear leads God's people into trouble, not into His arms. Fear is a lack of faith.

37–38. MOABITES . . . PEOPLE OF AMMON: The Moabites and Ammonites became two of Israel's fiercest and most persistent enemies. Lot's flirtation with the world— concluding with the incestuous immorality of his daughters—ultimately led to suffering and warfare for God's people for many generations to come.

⤳ FIRST IMPRESSIONS ⤳

1. When Abram and Lot separated, why did Lot choose to go down into the valley? What does this show about his priorities?

2. How did Abram's choices affect others? How did Lot's? Give specific examples.

3. Why did God destroy Sodom and Gomorrah in the first place? Was He justified in doing so?

4. How did Lot end up committing incest with his daughters? Trace the steps that led him to that situation, beginning at his separation from Abram.

⌇ Some Key Principles ⌇

Our actions have far-reaching impact in the lives of others.

Abram and Lot made very different decisions about where to live and what lifestyle to adopt, and those decisions influenced both of their families—and the entire nation of Israel—for hundreds of years to come.

This is a principle that we find reiterated throughout Scripture: our obedience or disobedience will affect the lives of others in ways that we cannot foresee. The ultimate example of this, of course, is in the life of the Lord Himself, whose complete and perfect obedience to the Father's will affected the lives of every person who has ever lived—and who ever will.

It is easy sometimes to think that some little point of disobedience or some small indulgence in sin will be harmless—"just this once." But we do not know what long-ranging impact that compromising decision may have in the lives of others.

The comforts of the world can become a deadly trap.

Lot did not leave Abram and head straight for a new house in Sodom; he arrived there by degrees. So it is with the comforts and entanglements of the world: they grow upon us a little at a time.

This is a difficult balance, because the Lord's people are called to be in the world but not of the world. We have no choice but to live in society and take part in the workaday economy, yet we must also be on guard to ensure that these entanglements do not become the focus of our lives.

"Do not love the world or the things in the world. If anyone loves the world, the love of the Father is not in him. For all that is in the world—the lust of the flesh, the lust of the eyes, and the pride of life—is not of the Father but is of the world. And the world is passing away, and the lust of it; but he who does the will of God abides forever" (1 John 2:15–17).

God does not condone sexual perversion, including the so-called "gay lifestyle."

God's judgment fell upon Sodom because the people of that city had given themselves over to sexual perversion and other forms of self-indulgence. The Bible warns again and again that those who indulge in sexual immorality will not inherit the kingdom of God (e.g., 1 Corinthians 6:9).

The world today teaches that sexual immorality is actually acceptable, normal, and even healthy. In fact, the concept of "immorality" itself has all but disappeared from the thinking of the common man. Even the definition of marriage itself is under attack from the world today. Yet God is emphatic that any form of sexual intercourse outside the sacred bonds of marriage is considered immoral and destructive. This includes fornication, adultery, homosexuality, and any other sexual activity that is not between a man and his wife.

We must not allow ourselves to be deceived by the lies of the world in this matter. God's people are absolutely forbidden to engage in sexual activity apart from the bonds of marriage, regardless of what nice-sounding names the world may give to those activities. The history of Sodom stands as a solemn warning on how seriously the Lord takes these matters.

The teachings of the world can corrupt the thinking of even God's people.

Lot demonstrated this concept in the way he interacted with the lust-driven maniacs of Sodom. A mob of rapists assailed his door, and he stepped outside and tried to reason with the crowd. He tried to appeal to their sense of goodness and propriety—even though they had none. He even went so far as to offer his own virgin daughters to be raped to death by the madmen. Lot was also driven by fear rather than faith—fear he invented for himself that had no basis in reality.

These are examples of how his thinking had been corrupted by the philosophies of Sodom. He had come to believe that the godly must compromise with the ungodly, that reason and logic could overcome the lust of the flesh, and that God would not protect him even after He had promised to do so.

It is not surprising that the world instills these same attitudes in Christians today. The thinking, values, and presuppositions of the world around us will seep into our own attitudes and priorities if we do not stand always on guard against it. "Do not be conformed to this world, but be transformed by the renewing of your mind, that you may prove what is that good and acceptable and perfect will of God" (Romans 12:1–2). "Keep your heart with all diligence, for out of it spring the issues of life" (Proverbs 4:23).

∽ DIGGING DEEPER ∽

5. *What does the world teach concerning homosexuality? How do those teachings compare with the Bible's teachings? How do you respond to this conflict?*

6. Second Peter 2:7–8 tells us that Lot was a righteous man. How do you reconcile that with his choices and actions in these passages? How can a righteous man sink to such depths?

7. When have you discovered that the world's values or presuppositions have worked their way into your own attitudes? How did you correct your thinking?

8. When have you seen an unexpected side effect of your own actions in someone else's life—with bad results? With good results?

⋋ TAKING IT PERSONALLY ⋌

9. What comforts of the world threaten to interfere with your own Christian walk? What needs to change in your life to guard against this danger?

10. In your own mind, identify the area or areas of sexual purity with which you face the greatest struggle or temptation. What does God's Word say about those sins? How can His Word strengthen you this week?

～ 4 ～
A Son of Promise

⌁ HISTORICAL BACKGROUND ⌁

Time has passed once again, and we now revisit Abraham after the birth of his promised son, Isaac. It is not entirely clear just how much time passed, and we don't know exactly how old Abraham and Isaac were. It seems likely that Isaac was somewhere between fourteen and twenty-one, which means that Abraham was well over one hundred years old.

Abraham, Sarah, and Isaac were evidently living in Beersheba at this point, along with the many people in Abraham's extended household. Abraham had undoubtedly been taking great delight in the company of his son, teaching him in the ways of the Lord and preparing him to take over as head of the great household one day.

There is a very unique bond that develops between a father and his son, and this relationship is the centerpiece in the passage that we will look at in this study. A son carries on his father's name and his father's goals and aspirations. A father is eager to pass on his knowledge and wisdom to his son. For Abraham, this bond was even more significant because Isaac was the son whom had long been promised by God, and it was through Isaac that God's greater promises of a great nation of descendants would be fulfilled. Furthermore, Abraham was more than a hundred years old; there was no possibility, from a human perspective, that he would ever have another child.

So imagine how shocked Abraham must have been one day when God suddenly appeared to him and told him to put his son Isaac to death! Isaac, the very son who had been promised by God for so many years, the one through whom Abraham was to produce a great nation that would be more numerous than the stars! How could God's promise come to pass if Isaac died so young?

Yet God's purposes are always bigger than we can understand, and there are times when He calls His people to do things that make no logical sense to our finite minds. At such times, we must imitate Abraham: trust and obey.

⤳ READING GENESIS 22:1–19 ⤳

A FINAL EXAM: *Abraham's promised son had finally arrived, and Isaac was growing up. Suddenly, God came to Abraham with the most difficult test of his life.*

1. AFTER THESE THINGS: Abraham was now well over a century old, and his son Isaac was at least in his early teens—fourteen or so at the youngest, perhaps as old as young manhood.

GOD TESTED ABRAHAM: The Hebrew word for "tested" is used of assaying metals. God was testing the quality and strength of Abraham's faith, just as a metallurgist tests the purity and temper of gold.

2. YOUR SON, YOUR ONLY SON ISAAC, WHOM YOU LOVE: Notice the strong reiterations of love and costliness in this phrase: "your son," "your only son," "whom you love." It is as though the Lord was letting Abraham know that He understood just how painful and costly this would be. Indeed, this is precisely what the Lord was doing, because He Himself would one day undergo the same torture—and His Son would actually go through with the sacrifice.

THE LAND OF MORIAH: This is probably the same Mount Moriah in Jerusalem where Solomon would later build the temple. (See 2 Chronicles 3:1.) It is a significant landmark, a place where the Lord repeatedly revealed Himself to His people, where the Jews would worship and sacrifice for hundreds of years. Today, this site is occupied by the Dome of the Rock, a Muslim temple that encloses a large outcropping of natural stone—which is still claimed as the site of Abraham's intended sacrifice of Isaac.

OFFER HIM THERE AS A BURNT OFFERING: This command would be startling enough in any circumstances, but in Abraham's case it was doubly so: the loss of Isaac would mean that God's promise of innumerable heirs—more than the sand of the sea-shore—would be cut short and fail. Yet, as we will see, Abraham was so convinced of God's faithfulness to His promise that he knew that Isaac could not be permanently taken away from him.

ABRAHAM'S RESPONSE: *God's command makes no logical sense—how could His promise come to pass if Abraham obeyed? Yet that is exactly what Abraham did.*

3. SO ABRAHAM. . . : It is interesting that Sarah does not appear in this historical account. We must resist the modern temptation of suggesting that she is omitted because of some male chauvinism on the part of Moses, as though he didn't think that a woman's perspective mattered. She does not appear in this account because the Holy Spirit was

36

motivating Moses on what to include and exclude, and His purpose was to give us not only an account of a historical event, but also a picture of an event that is yet to come—the sacrifice of the Son of God—the final sacrifice for sin—by His own Father.

ABRAHAM ROSE EARLY IN THE MORNING: When we are called upon by God to do something that is difficult or costly, it is always best to set about obeying as quickly as possible.

HE SPLIT THE WOOD FOR THE BURNT OFFERING: The area around Jerusalem, the most likely site of Moriah, was probably wooded in the time of Abraham. It might seem odd that he would carry split firewood for three days' journey if he could have collected it there, but Abraham was not permitting himself any opportunity for a change of heart once he got there. Further, Abraham's advance preparations remind us of the fact that God began preparing to sacrifice His own Son on the day when Adam sinned—indeed, before the very foundation of the world.

4. ON THE THIRD DAY: God had commanded Abraham to travel to a distant mountain for the sacrifice, which at first glance seems odd, since there were plenty of high places near Beersheba where he was living. Yet one part of God's reason may well be the fact that it would require a three-day journey to get there, thereby providing a picture of the death and resurrection of Christ. It is also significant that this location would one day be the place where Abraham's descendants would build the temple—a place where sacrifices took place continually.

ARRIVING AT MORIAH: *After three days' travel, Abraham and Isaac arrived at the place of sacrifice. The moment of truth was at hand.*

ABRAHAM LIFTED HIS EYES: Here we see this important phrase again, which we first noted when Lot "lifted his eyes" and looked upon the good things that the world had to offer. (See Genesis 13:10 in Study 3.) In stark contrast to Lot, Abraham lifted his eyes and looked upon the horrific sacrifice that lay before him. In the same way, the Lord Himself would later "set His face like flint" as He also went to Jerusalem to be offered up in sacrifice. (See Isaiah 50:7 and Luke 9:51.)

5. THE LAD AND I WILL GO: This sacrifice was intimately and solely between father and son, and nobody else was invited to participate. In the same way, the final sacrifice of God's own Son was provided and paid solely by God Himself; no man could offer any element of the atonement.

WE WILL COME BACK TO YOU: Here again we see the absolute faith and confidence that Abraham was placing in God. He knew that God would certainly fulfill His promise to make a great nation out of Isaac and was therefore completely confident that he would return again with his son. Yet he was also anticipating that he would have to put his son to death. Through absolute faith in God's promise, he was "concluding that God [was] able to raise [Isaac] up, even from the dead" (Hebrews 11:19).

CLIMBING MOUNT MORIAH: *The parallels between Isaac and Jesus now become startling, as the son of promise climbs the mount to be offered up in sacrifice.*

6. LAID IT ON ISAAC HIS SON: The father laid the burden on the shoulders of his son, just as God the Father would later do with His Son: "the LORD has laid on Him the iniquity of us all" (Isaiah 53:6). Isaac also typifies Christ in a much more literal way, as he carried the very wood that was to devour his body in sacrifice, even as Christ carried His own cross to Calvary. (See John 19:17.)

HE TOOK THE FIRE IN HIS HAND, AND A KNIFE: These two symbols of God's wrath forcibly remind us of the very reason why a sacrifice was necessary in the first place: God's wrath and judgment against man's sin had to be appeased. Jesus bore the full brunt of God's justice as He hung upon the cross, and His Father struck Him dead with His own hand. Imagine the emotions that must have surged through Abraham's breast as he carried in his own hand the very weapons he was about to use against his son. This picture can help us understand a small portion of what it cost God—Father and Son—to pay for our sins.

THE TWO OF THEM WENT TOGETHER: Here again we see a heartrending picture of the perfect obedience of the son to his father, just as Christ was fully obedient to His Father. The two walked together in complete unity, Father and Son equally devoted to redeeming mankind from sin and death.

7. ISAAC SPOKE TO ABRAHAM HIS FATHER: Isaac was at least fourteen years old, and perhaps in his twenties, while Abraham was a centenarian and undoubtedly beginning to grow frail. Isaac could easily have resisted his father's intentions had he chosen to do so, and his question here suggests that he had a good idea of what his father intended to do. Yet Isaac asked only once and then complied without any further comment. This picture, once again, was completed in Christ Himself, who prayed, "Father, if it is Your will, take this cup away from Me; nevertheless not My will, but Yours, be done" (Luke 22:42).

8. GOD WILL PROVIDE FOR HIMSELF THE LAMB FOR A BURNT OFFERING: The presence of a sacrificial lamb, which served as a substitute for Isaac, again typifies the substitutionary sacrifice of Christ, who died in the place of sinners who deserved to die. This statement also demonstrates the fullness of Abraham's faith.

9. Abraham built an altar: Once again we see Abraham building an altar to the Lord—but this time his sacrifice and worship would be extremely costly to himself. This is the ultimate act of worship, to sacrifice something that is very precious out of obedience to God and faith in His promises. A lifetime of practice in building altars and worshiping God had prepared Abraham for this fateful moment.

he bound Isaac his son and laid him on the altar: Once again we have a moving picture of God the Father, who would one day lay His own Son on the cross. It is left to our own imaginations to picture the anguish that Abraham must have been feeling at this moment, an agony that could not compare with what the Father endured when His Son was crucified.

10. Abraham stretched out his hand and took the knife to slay his son: What a dramatic moment! Abraham demonstrated to the uttermost his absolute determination to obey God, even to the point of sacrificing his own son. His obedience and faith provide a complete picture of the sacrifice of God's Son on the cross and offer another confirmation of the truth of the Gospels, that Jesus is indeed the Messiah and the only begotten Son of God. We would have been deprived of this Old Testament picture if Abraham had balked at any point in his obedience or obeyed only partially—as at previous times in his life.

Stop!: *Suddenly God intervened to hold Abraham back from the final act of sacrifice. Abraham had passed his final test, providing a stunning portrait of Christ's future sufferings.*

---

12. now I know that you fear God: God's purposes in our lives have many facets, and we cannot know fully what He intends. Here we discover that part of God's purpose in this test was to prove, once and for all, the complete extent of Abraham's devotion to the Lord. We also know that He intended this test to be a picture of His final redemption to come, yet Abraham was not told this. Our place is to trust and obey, even when we cannot see God's purposes in life's circumstances.

you have not withheld your son: Abraham demonstrated through his actions that his love and reverence for God superseded even his deepest human relationships. Moreover, as a picture of Christ, this statement looks forward to the fact that God would not withhold His only Son in redeeming mankind from sin. "Greater love has no one than this, than to lay down one's life for his friends" (John 15:13). "For God so loved the world that He gave His only begotten Son, that whoever believes in Him should not perish but have everlasting life" (John 3:16).

13. ABRAHAM LIFTED HIS EYES: Once again we encounter this meaningful phrase, and this time Abraham's eyes beheld that which filled his heart with joy—a direct contrast to the last time he "lifted his eyes" and beheld the coming death of his son. Now he discovered that God had provided a sacrifice to take Isaac's place, and we can be assured that Abraham's heart was filled with overwhelming relief.

A BURNT OFFERING INSTEAD OF HIS SON: The truth that God is demonstrating here is that no man can offer a sacrifice that will atone for his own sins—never mind the sins of others. If we are to be forgiven, our sins must be paid by a perfect substitute. Only Christ's perfect sacrifice could accomplish that, the final sacrifice that God Himself provided for mankind. Jesus gave Himself as that sacrifice, dying on the cross in your place and mine to pay the final price for our sins.

REITERATING THE PROMISE: *With a covenant that can never be broken, God once again swore that He would make Abraham's descendants into a great nation.*

14. THE-LORD-WILL-PROVIDE: This is a lesson that Abraham had to learn in his own life, as indeed most Christians must learn as well. We will see in a future study that Abraham attempted to provide for himself an heir—with disastrous results—rather than waiting for God to provide the fulfillment to His promises. "And my God shall supply all your need according to His riches in glory by Christ Jesus" (Philippians 4:19).

IN THE MOUNT OF THE LORD IT SHALL BE PROVIDED: The Mount of the Lord refers to Mount Zion in Jerusalem, the center of Jewish worship. This promise was fulfilled when God's Son climbed another mountain outside of Jerusalem called Mount Calvary, and the promise will be completely fulfilled when God establishes His New Jerusalem. (See Revelation 3, 21.) On Calvary, God provided the final atonement for the sin of mankind.

16. BY MYSELF I HAVE SWORN: "For when God made a promise to Abraham, because He could swear by no one greater, He swore by Himself" (Hebrews 6:13).

17. YOUR DESCENDANTS SHALL POSSESS THE GATE OF THEIR ENEMIES: This metaphor means that the descendants of Abraham would conquer and control their enemies, but it also had an interesting and very literal fulfillment in Samson. (See Judges 16.)

✄ FIRST IMPRESSIONS ✄

1. Put yourself in Abraham's place. How would you have reacted when God commanded you to sacrifice Isaac? What would you have done?

2. What were God's reasons for commanding Abraham to do this? What were Abraham's reasons for obeying?

3. Why did God send Abraham to Moriah rather than just have him perform the sacrifice near where he was living?

4. Why was Isaac so cooperative?

⌒ Some Key Principles ⌒

God sometimes calls us to costly obedience.

There is no question that Abraham was severely tested by God's command to sacrifice his beloved son. Yet God is not frivolous; this command was not just some random test. His purpose was to prove the strength of Abraham's faith—and a great deal more. He also wanted to present to the world a picture of His plan to sacrifice His own Son on the cross.

He will sometimes ask His children, even in modern times, to obey Him in ways that are very costly. The principle He wants us to learn is that faith-filled obedience is more valuable than anything this world has to offer.

The other side to this principle, however, is that costly obedience leads to eternal riches. Abraham's obedience brought a priceless blessing to the entire world, showing mankind just how much God was willing to do to redeem us from death. Our Savior Himself was willing to obey at any cost, and we must be willing to follow His example.

God never gives us tests that we cannot pass.

God "knows our frame; He remembers that we are dust" (Psalm 103:14). He sends tests into our lives in order to strengthen us, to build Christlike character in our lives—not to find fault with us or to seek an excuse to punish us. His tests are designed for us to pass, not to fail.

Of course, when we are in the middle of a trial, it can seem overwhelming and unbearable. At such times, we must remember that Christians have God's Holy Spirit within us, working right alongside us to help us through the trials and tribulations of life. There are times when we are called upon merely to endure and to trust the Lord, to accept a trial or hardship as from the hand of God without trying to manipulate our own way out of it.

"No temptation has overtaken you except such as is common to man; but God is faithful, who will not allow you to be tempted beyond what you are able, but with the temptation will also make the way of escape, that you may be able to bear it" (1 Corinthians 10:13).

God's sacrifice for our sins was costly to both Father and Son.

It is interesting to notice that the focus of this passage is on Abraham rather than on Isaac. At first glance this may seem strange; after all, it was Isaac who was going to die, not Abraham! But one reason for this is that it gives us a picture of what it cost God the Father to send His only begotten Son to die—slowly and painfully—on the cross at Calvary.

Abraham's long wait for the birth of his beloved son helps us remember how much the Father did to bring His planned Redeemer into our world—only to have Him die a horrible death. Abraham's pain over sacrificing Isaac was nothing compared to what the Father endured when His sinless Son became sin's sacrifice on our behalf.

The cooperation of Isaac and the unity of father and son in this passage are mere glimpses of the perfect unity of the Godhead: Father, Son, and Holy Spirit. And what is most amazing of all is the fact that our God did all this just for the sake of bringing reconciliation with us, sinners in rebellion against Him. We do serve a great and loving God!

ᕲ DIGGING DEEPER ᕲ

5. *In what ways does the sacrifice of Isaac illustrate the sacrifice of Christ? Be specific.*

6. *Even though Isaac was not sacrificed, what did this ordeal cost Abraham? What did he gain from it? What did others gain?*

7. How might things have been different if Abraham had not obeyed God? How did God know that Abraham would obey?

8. How did Abraham know that God would not permanently take Isaac from him? On what did Abraham build his faith?

✒ TAKING IT PERSONALLY ✒

9. When has God called you to costly obedience? How did you respond? Is there an area of obedience that He is calling you to today?

10. In what ways might God be testing you at present? How can the Holy Spirit provide comfort and strength? Who can you ask for prayer support?

5
JACOB AND ESAU

⌁ HISTORICAL BACKGROUND ⌁

We now move forward in time to the latter years of Isaac's life. His wife Rebekah was barren, and Isaac pleaded with the Lord to open her womb—which He did in duplicate! Rebekah discovered that she had twin boys wrestling inside her, and the Lord prophesied concerning their future.

At the time of these events, Isaac was growing old and infirm. He had already lost his eyesight, and he anticipated that his life was drawing to its close (though it wasn't). He and his family were probably living in Beersheba, where Isaac had spent much of his childhood with Abraham.

An important element in these passages has to do with the birthright of the eldest son. This birthright involved a double portion of the inheritance when the father died, and it also brought a very special blessing from father to son. This blessing was at least as important as the material inheritance, and in Isaac's case, it was the most important element.

The birthright almost invariably was reserved for the firstborn son; only in very special circumstances was it bestowed on another. It was considered a very valuable right, something the firstborn son would treasure and insist upon as his by birth. It could, however, be bought and sold if a firstborn son were foolish enough to part with it.

This topic is of significance to Christians today, because we inherit the birthright of Jesus, God's only begotten Son. This heritage is beyond price; it includes our eternal life in the presence of God the Father.

⌁ READING GENESIS 25:21–34 ⌁

TWIN NATIONS: *Rebekah was healed of her barrenness and conceived two boys. The Lord then came to her with a word of prophecy concerning their future.*

22. THE CHILDREN STRUGGLED TOGETHER WITHIN HER: Esau would be the firstborn of the twins, with Jacob following immediately after. This struggle that began in the womb would continue between these twin brothers for the rest of their lives.

23. Two nations are in your womb: Esau's descendants were the Edomites, who caused problems for the Israelites on and off throughout the Old Testament period. Jacob would become the father of the twelve tribes of Israel after his own name was changed from Jacob to Israel.

THE OLDER SHALL SERVE THE YOUNGER: Notice that this prophecy made no mention of the birthright of the elder son; it merely predicted that the elder would serve the younger. The implication is that the Lord's favor would rest with the younger son, but it did not touch upon which son *should* receive the birthright. See notes on verse 32 below for more on the birthright.

HAIRY AND HEEL-GRABBER: *The sons were born, the first one with lots of hair and the second one grabbing his heel. This heel-grabbing tendency would plague Jacob for most of his life.*

---

25. RED: A ruddy complexion was apparently not common among the Old Testament Jews—although David is also described as "ruddy and good-looking" (1 Samuel 17:42). Some have suggested that Esau's ruddy complexion and hairy body were signs of an excessively passionate nature or a tendency toward cruelty. Esau's adult lifestyle lends some credence to this idea, although the text says nothing to this effect.

ESAU: Probably means "hairy."

26. TOOK HOLD OF ESAU'S HEEL: This gesture would become typical of Jacob's life, as he grew up to be a grasping and conniving person. It is also an interesting foreshadowing of the way he would gain his brother's birthright.

JACOB: Means "heel catcher" or "supplanter."

28. ISAAC LOVED ESAU . . . BUT REBEKAH LOVED JACOB: Here we find the beginning of problems, as the parents chose favorites.

MY SOUL FOR SOME STEW: *Esau came home from hunting, feeling very tired and hungry. And Jacob was waiting for him. In this shocking passage, Esau demonstrated the foolish short-sightedness of his value system.*

---

29. JACOB COOKED A STEW: We are not told what Jacob's motives were in cooking this stew at this strategic moment. It is possible that he was innocently making his own supper, yet it is also possible that he planned to tempt his brother, who would be returning shortly from the hunt. In light of Jacob's future acts of cunning, it is quite possible that he had planned in advance to barter for his brother's birthright.

HE WAS WEARY: It is when we are weary—physically or spiritually—that we must be on our guard the most. When our strength is down, so is our ability to recognize and resist temptation.

30. PLEASE FEED ME: This is a very legitimate request, insofar as it goes. It is not presumptuous to ask a brother for help in time of need. The problem for Esau, however, is that he would allow his immediate hunger to become a devouring lust.

RED STEW: The Hebrew for this phrase can be transliterated as "red red." This was probably a lentil stew.

HIS NAME WAS CALLED EDOM: This is comparable to "Red," a common enough nickname for redheaded persons even today. Esau's ruddy complexion would have lent itself to this nickname to begin with, but his name will forever become associated with the dreadful decision he was about to make. This episode made the name Edom remain with him throughout his life, and his descendants were the Edomites.

31. SELL ME YOUR BIRTHRIGHT: See verse 32 for an explanation on birthrights. God has already prophesied that "the older shall serve the younger" (verse 23), but Jacob was evidently not willing to wait for God to bring this about. By bartering for his brother's birthright, Jacob hoped to switch places with him, making himself equivalent to the firstborn and placing Esau in a subservient position. Jacob would spend much of his adult life learning to trust in God's promises rather than manipulating the circumstances himself.

32. I AM ABOUT TO DIE: Esau was *not* about to die; he was merely hungry and tired. But a habit of immediate gratification caused him to magnify his urges into life-threatening calamities. Esau was evidently accustomed to taking what he needed and satisfying his appetites quickly. This is also a common problem in modern society, where we specialize in instant gratification. Christians are exhorted to deny the flesh in order to prevent our fleshly desires from ruling our lives.

WHAT IS THIS BIRTHRIGHT TO ME?: The birthright was a sacred treasure to the firstborn male in Jacob's time. It afforded the firstborn son a double portion of the inheritance when his father died. It also meant that the father would pronounce a special blessing upon his firstborn son and his descendants. We should remember that Isaac did not own any land in Canaan, so Esau's inheritance probably did not seem particularly significant to him at this moment. The bigger and more important portion of his birthright was the spiritual blessing that Isaac would pass on to his son, and this is what Esau was about to spurn.

34. HE ATE AND DRANK, AROSE, AND WENT HIS WAY: Esau will forever epitomize the man who satisfies his physical needs without any concern for his soul.

THUS ESAU DESPISED HIS BIRTHRIGHT: He placed more value on the immediate gratification of his physical appetites than he did on the long-range spiritual blessings that were his by right. The full weight of this folly would come home to Esau very soon when he got hungry again. He sold something invaluable for something very temporary. It is hard to believe that anyone could make such a foolish bargain—yet God's people do the very same thing when we willfully indulge our fleshly lusts, thereby spurning God's grace and treating His Son's redemption with contempt. We are, in effect, despising our own birthright. "Pursue . . . holiness, without which no one will see the Lord: looking carefully lest anyone fall short of the grace of God; . . . lest there be any fornicator or profane person like Esau, who for one morsel of food sold his birthright. For you know that afterward, when he wanted to inherit the blessing, he was rejected, for he found no place for repentance, though he sought it diligently with tears" (Hebrews 12:14–17).

⏴ READING GENESIS 27:1–38 ⏵

FAMILY PLOT: *Rebekah now conspires with Jacob to deceive Isaac and steal the birthright from Esau. In this sordid story, the entire family acts badly.*

2. I DO NOT KNOW THE DAY OF MY DEATH: Isaac actually lived another forty-three years after this event.

4. MAKE ME SAVORY FOOD: Here we discover a pattern, as Isaac himself fell into trouble through a pot of savory stew.

THAT MY SOUL MAY BLESS YOU BEFORE I DIE: Like his son Esau, Isaac was consumed with the urge to satisfy his physical appetites. Esau claimed that he was about to die when he was merely hungry; Isaac made a very similar leap in logic here, as though his death were imminent or his blessing dependent upon having an immediate bowl of venison stew. Some have claimed that Isaac was out of God's will in his desire to bestow the blessings of birthright upon Esau, but we must remember that the prophecy concerning the brothers was that the "older shall serve the younger" (25:23)—not that the younger would receive the birthright inheritance.

8. OBEY MY VOICE: This phrase shows up repeatedly in the book of Genesis, frequently with negative implications. Adam listened to the voice of his wife and ate the forbidden fruit (3:17). Later he heard the voice of the Lord in the garden of Eden and hid himself (3:10). Abram heeded the voice of his wife and produced a son through Hagar—against the Lord's will (16:2). Here we find Rebekah giving ungodly advice to her son, and he "gave heed" to her words.

10. THAT HE MAY BLESS YOU BEFORE HIS DEATH: Rebekah may have been thinking of the prophecy concerning her sons—that the older would serve the younger—and perhaps she was suddenly filled with fear. Her husband was about to bestow the blessing on the wrong son! It is equally possible, however, that she concocted this scheme simply because Jacob was her favorite. Whatever her motives, her actions were wicked. God's will is not accomplished by mankind's devious schemes.

12. I SHALL SEEM TO BE A DECEIVER TO HIM: The irony of this statement is almost humorous. Jacob was essentially afraid that he would be caught, discovered to be exactly what he was: a base deceiver of his own father. His son Joseph would later demonstrate the correct approach to such temptations by declaring, "How then can I do this great wickedness, and sin against God?" (Genesis 39:9).

13. LET YOUR CURSE BE ON ME: It is possible that Rebekah was acting on a firm conviction that Jacob would be blessed and not cursed, yet her actions were still wrong. We are not to use God's promises to take advantage of others for our own profit. Furthermore, each man is responsible for his own actions; the consequences of Jacob's actions would fall to Jacob, not to his mother—whether she liked it or not.

19. I AM ESAU YOUR FIRSTBORN: If we have in any way minimized the sin of Jacob and Rebekah previously, there can be no justification any longer—regardless of the Lord's prophecy concerning the birthright. Jacob was lying outright to his own father— blind with the infirmity of old age—claiming to be Esau, saying that the goat stew was actually venison that he had recently taken in the hunt, and disguising his very body with goat hair to mimic his brother's hairy skin.

20. THE LORD YOUR GOD BROUGHT IT TO ME: Jacob's treachery is breathtaking, that he would have the effrontery to claim that God was involved in his wicked deception of his aged father. Yet here, too, we are forced to recognize that God's people still act in this manner today. "The heart is deceitful above all things, and desperately wicked" (Jeremiah 17:9), and it is very easy to justify our own willful actions as being motivated by God's leading. "Let no one say when he is tempted, 'I am tempted by God'; for God cannot be tempted by evil, nor does He Himself tempt anyone. But each one is tempted when he is drawn away by his own desires and enticed" (James 1:13–14).

THE STOLEN BLESSING: *Isaac was finally convinced by Jacob's outright lies, and he bestowed the blessing of birthright upon him. He also showed, however, that he had forgotten the Lord's prophecy.*

29. BE MASTER OVER YOUR BRETHREN: Isaac himself was not without some culpability in this sordid event, for he certainly understood the Lord's prophecy concerning his sons, which included the fact that Esau and his descendants would serve Jacob, not vice versa. He must also have been aware that Esau had sold the birthright to Jacob, and for better or worse, that was a binding contract—Isaac was as bound to recognize it as Esau was. Furthermore, Esau had married Canaanite women (see Genesis 26:34–35), which had brought much grief to his parents. In many ways, Isaac should have realized that Jacob had been chosen of God, and this blessing ought to have gone to him.

CURSED BE EVERYONE WHO CURSES YOU, AND BLESSED BE THOSE WHO BLESS YOU: This may be a stock bit of phrasing in the blessings that fathers bestowed upon their sons, yet it is almost verbatim the blessing that the Lord bestowed upon Abraham. It suggests that Isaac was expecting the chosen seed to continue through Esau—perhaps through both Esau and Jacob. But Esau had already removed himself from that plan by selling his birthright.

WEEPING WON'T BRING IT BACK: *Esau finally came face-to-face with the monumental folly he had committed by selling his birthright. In many ways he is a picture of those who reject Christ.*

---

35. TAKEN AWAY YOUR BLESSING: Esau did receive a blessing from his father, but it was not the blessing of birthright. There can be only one such blessing, and once bestowed, it can never be removed. This aspect of the birthright blessing is a wonderful picture of the security of our birthright as Christians. Our rebirth into the family of Christ brings us all the blessings of His birthright as the only begotten Son of God—and this inheritance and blessing can never be taken away from us.

38. ESAU LIFTED UP HIS VOICE AND WEPT: Realizing the irrevocable nature of what had happened, Esau responded with both anger and grief. Like Esau, those who reject the spiritual birthright that God offers through His Son Jesus Christ will also one day weep over the irreversible consequences of their rejection. When we accept Christ's atonement for our sins, we are brought into the family of God, and we inherit the full blessing and birthright of the Son of God. But there will come a day when those who have rejected this gift will be cast "into the furnace of fire. There will be wailing and gnashing of teeth" (Matthew 13:42).

⤳ FIRST IMPRESSIONS ⤳

1. *Why might Esau have been so willing to sell his birthright? Why did he not consider it valuable?*

2. Why did Jacob play such a trick on his brother, just for the sake of the birthright?

3. Whose sin is worse in your opinion: Jacob's or Esau's? Why?

4. If you had been in Isaac's position, how would you have responded to Jacob and Rebekah's conspiracy?

ᕈ Some Key Principles ᕈ

The birthright of Jesus is eternal life.

Every human on earth is born from the seed of Adam, and that means that every one of us is under the curse of sin and death. But God sent His Son to bring us a "new birth," allowing us to be "born again" into the family of God. When we do this, we immediately receive the full blessing and birthright that the Father has in store for His Son—and this includes eternal life and freedom from the curse of death.

But this birthright is only passed on to those who are of the family of God, who have been born again into faith in Jesus Christ. It is, therefore, entirely possible to miss the opportunity, to treat this birthright with contempt as though it were not even as valuable as temporal pleasure or immediate gratification. This may not be the conscious train of logic that people have in mind when they refuse to accept Christ, but it is, in fact, what they are doing.

We must never treat God's grace with contempt, lest we become like Esau, who treated his own birthright with such derision. In the end, he realized his dreadful mistake—but he realized too late. He could not buy it back, even with weeping and anguish. If you accomplish nothing else in life, make sure you don't miss out on the birthright of eternal life through Jesus Christ. We must not be like "Esau, who for one morsel of food sold his birthright. For you know that afterward, when he wanted to inherit the blessing, he was rejected, for he found no place for repentance, though he sought it diligently with tears" (Hebrews 12:16–17).

God's purposes are not furthered by our manipulative schemes.

God had intended from the beginning that Esau be subservient to Jacob; He promised it before the boys were born, and He would have accomplished it *without* any plots from Isaac's family. We saw the same principle in the life of Abraham: he had God's promise of an heir through his wife Sarah, yet he allowed his fears (and his wife's schemes) to override his faith in God's word.

In each of these cases, the schemes of men led to very bad consequences. Jacob's schemes alienated him from his twin brother for the rest of his life and led to his being deceived repeatedly by others. Abraham's involvement with Hagar led to a deep-seated enmity between Arabs and Israelis that is very much alive, even today.

God accomplishes what He promises. This does not mean that we are not involved in those promises, but our involvement requires *obedience*, not scheming. Our involvement may sometimes require no effort at all on our part—except for placing our faith in God's provision. Indeed, this effort often proves the most difficult, as we have seen in this study.

The pleasures and cares of this world are very temporary, but God's blessings are eternal.

Esau possessed something that had tremendous long-term value in the blessing of his father, a blessing that carries down even into modern times. Yet he sold this priceless blessing for something that lasted less than a day; within a few hours, Esau was probably hungry again.

The world offers countless pleasures and opportunities and distractions, and life brings many forms of sorrow, suffering, and worry—but none of these things will last. We must be always on our guard so that we do not behave like Esau, letting go of the priceless relationship we have with the Father in exchange for some fleeting sensual pleasure. Further, we should never allow the sorrows and cares of this world to persuade us that God is not involved, that He does not care about His children, or that He has forgotten His promises.

The Christian's birthright is to enjoy the intimacy with the Father that Jesus Himself enjoys—perfect and complete and eternally secure. We must remember the example of Esau and take care to not exchange that for anything in the world.

⌒ DIGGING DEEPER ⌒

5. *Consider each member of Isaac's family. What led each to doubt or forget God's word? To treat His promises with contempt?*

Isaac:

Jacob:

Esau:

Rebekah:

6. *What were Esau's top priorities? What were Jacob's? Rebekah's? Isaac's?*

7. *How do you resolve Jacob's lies and deceit with the fact that he was chosen by God to bring about the line of Christ?*

8. What did each person in the family lose in the passages we've studied? What did each gain?

Person	Lost	Gained
Isaac:		
Rebekah:		
Esau:		
Jacob:		

❧ Taking It Personally ❧

9. Have you accepted the birthright of eternal life through Jesus? If not, what is holding you back?

10. What is your top priority in life at present? What things are hindering or endangering your relationship with God?

Section 2:

Characters

In This Section:

~ 6 ~
ABRAHAM

↳ CHARACTER'S BACKGROUND ↲

We have been studying a number of important events in Abraham's life in order to get a bigger picture of the history surrounding the chosen people of God—leading to those of us who are adopted into the spiritual family of Abraham through the rebirth offered by Jesus. Now let's take a closer look at the man himself.

Abraham was called "the friend of God," and he was chosen directly by God to be the founding father of His chosen people. This naturally raises the question, why Abraham? What was so special about him that set him apart from the world around him? What did he do to deserve such honor?

The primary answer, of course, is *nothing*! Abraham did not "deserve" honor from God any more than we do; he was chosen by God through God's grace, not through his own merit. Yet God *grew* Abraham into a person of real merit, a man whose life is an example to us even today, thousands of years later. It is worthwhile to ask ourselves what it means to be a friend of God.

Abraham was, first and foremost, a man of faith. We have seen that in several of our previous studies as we witnessed Abraham believing God's promise for a son even when it seemed impossible. Then we watched him sacrifice that very son, convinced that God could raise him from the dead. Abraham was also a man of obedience, quick to do what the Lord commanded. And, fortunately for us, he was also a man of flesh—a man who sometimes *didn't* obey completely what the Lord told him to do. In this we can find encouragement and realize that God chooses ordinary people to be His friends, even those who fall short from time to time.

In this study, we will discover another aspect of Abraham's life that will give us added insight into being a friend of God: Abraham interceded for others. He received a personal visit from God Himself as the Lord was on His way with two angels to pour down judgment on Sodom and Gomorrah. Abraham could easily have minded his own business and "stayed out of it," allowing God to do what He thought best. He could have gone the other direction and felt proud that he was so much more righteous than those Sodomites. But instead, he humbly approached the Lord and began to plead for Him to withhold His righteous judgment from the cities of Sodom and Gomorrah.

Abraham's faith led to God's declaration that he was righteous, but that faith quite naturally worked itself out in deeds—and the two together encompass the righteousness of Abraham. The friend of God, we will see, was one who had both faith *and* works, since genuine faith results in heartfelt obedience.

⤳ Reading Genesis 18:1, 16–33 ⤳

Guess Who's Coming to Dinner?: *In this narrative, God came to Abraham and had dinner with him, accompanied by two angels. The angels then headed for Sodom, but God remained with Abraham to talk.*

1. the Lord appeared to him: Abraham was seated by his tent when three men appeared. One of those men was God Himself, appearing in human form. Abraham invited the men to dine with him, and the Lord conversed with Abraham and Sarah about their promised son. (Isaac had not yet been born.)

16. rose from there and looked toward Sodom: Abraham was living in Mamre at this point (see the map in the Introduction). The exact locations of Sodom and Gomorrah are not known, but they were probably situated at the southern tip of what is now the Dead Sea (or Salt Sea). Mamre was located in the high hills above the Jordan Valley, and Sodom was perhaps twenty-five to thirty-five miles away.

Shall I Tell Him?: *Here we are given a privileged glimpse into God's mind as He sought to determine whether or not to reveal His plans—and His character—to His friend Abraham.*

17. Shall I hide from Abraham . . . ?: Here we are given a rare peek into the mind of God Himself. The question He asked was probably rhetorical, meaning, "Now that I have brought Abraham into my confidence, I cannot exclude him from this event."

18. all the nations of the earth shall be blessed in him: A very important part of this blessing that Abraham would bring upon the world was a clearer understanding of the character of God Himself. Prior to Abraham, God's direct interactions with men had been limited. But He was now planning to reveal more of Himself to Abraham and his descendants, and their role was to tell the world what He revealed. In this passage, God was going to reveal to Abraham another aspect of His character: justice. In addition to this, as we shall see, Abraham was about to learn what *his* role was in becoming a blessing to the nations.

19. I HAVE KNOWN HIM: The word *know* here implies a deep and intimate relationship. It is also used in Scripture to describe a husband's intimacy with his wife. God's relationship with Abraham was deeply intimate, and He understood Abraham better than Abraham understood himself.

IN ORDER THAT HE MAY COMMAND HIS CHILDREN: God here revealed the very reason why He had selected Abraham: in order that Abraham would "command" his entire household in the way of the Lord. It is significant that the Lord did not expect Abraham to *ask* or to *suggest* how his household should live; he was to *command* them. This implies that the head of the household should have a strong spiritual authority in the home. This concept goes against modern notions of marriage and child rearing, which teach us that children should be offered various options but allowed to choose their own "path." That is not the sort of leadership God expected of Abraham.

KEEP THE WAY OF THE LORD: God wanted Abraham to ensure that his household *kept* the way of the Lord, which implies that they might otherwise *lose* the way of the Lord. This has happened in Western society, as an entire generation is growing up without any knowledge of God's Word and God's ways. The Hebrew word translated "keep" here literally means "to hedge about with thorns." In other words, God is warning us that we must deliberately guard and protect "the way of the Lord" within our homes, lest our children and grandchildren lose the way.

TO DO RIGHTEOUSNESS AND JUSTICE: God was about to demonstrate both of these aspects of His character. He wanted His children to live righteously, which is *not* what the Sodomites were doing. Their wickedness was about to bring upon their own heads the justice of God. It is important to notice that He expects His people to exhibit both aspects of His character as well—both righteousness *and* justice.

GOD'S PLAN: *The Lord explained to Abraham why He had come—He was going to visit Sodom and Gomorrah to see whether they were as wicked as reported.*

20. THE OUTCRY AGAINST SODOM AND GOMORRAH IS GREAT: We saw in Study 3 the extent of Sodom's wickedness, as the entire city turned out and attempted to sodomize the very angels of God. Men tend to grow more wicked as they persuade themselves further that there is no God in heaven to hold them accountable. (This is one of the reasons that Satan has worked so hard to deceive modern mankind with the false belief of evolution.) But God let Abraham know here that He is always aware of our actions—good or bad—and that persistent wickedness raises an actual outcry before His throne in heaven.

21. I WILL GO DOWN NOW AND SEE: God went a step further than merely listening to the outcry against Sodom—He came in physical form to meet with Abraham and enact judgment on Sodom. When God comes to earth in the flesh, it is generally for the purpose of judgment. He came to the garden of Eden (Genesis 3) to confront Adam for committing the first sin. He came to Babel to investigate the great tower that men were building out of their colossal pride (Genesis 11). Ultimately, He would come to earth as a baby for the most costly act of judgment, and God's justice would fall fully upon the shoulders of His Son. In every case, however, God's visit is an act of grace and mercy, as He always goes beyond what is required.

22. THE MEN TURNED AWAY: The two angels who were with the Lord. We already met them in Study 3 when they appeared later in the day at the gate of Sodom.

ABRAHAM DRAWS NEAR: *God had treated Abraham with intimate friendship, and here Abraham responded. His first step was to take another step—nearer to God.*

ABRAHAM STILL STOOD BEFORE THE LORD: This is a sign of intimate friendship, a special relationship that even the angels do not share. Abraham stood almost as an equal before his Creator, speaking to Him face-to-face as one man speaks to another. Abraham had become God's personal friend.

23. ABRAHAM CAME NEAR: And now Abraham would take that intimacy one step farther and deliberately draw himself even closer to God. The Hebrew implies the deepest form of adoration and worship. This is the very reason that God chose Abraham to be His special envoy in the world; He wants His children to deliberately draw close to Him in worship and admiration.

WOULD YOU . . . ?: Abraham began a conversation with the Lord in which he interceded for Sodom, yet he was also trying to get to know God better. He was, in effect, asking God about His character, trying to understand the balance between justice and mercy, grace and judgment.

DESTROY THE RIGHTEOUS WITH THE WICKED: The following conversation reveals something priceless in the character of Abraham as he began to intercede for others. He was in a unique relationship with God, set apart from the world around him, and here he was, standing face-to-face with the Creator Himself! It would have been very easy for him to think of his own needs, but Abraham's concern was to know God and to intercede for others. Abraham began his intercession by effectively praying for Lot's safety, that he might not be destroyed along with the people of Sodom.

INTERCEDING FOR SODOM: *Abraham's nephew Lot was in Sodom, and it is not surprising that he interceded for his safety. But then Abraham went beyond that and interceded for the whole city.*

24. SUPPOSE THERE WERE FIFTY . . . : Abraham went farther than merely interceding for his family members; he began to pray for the people of Sodom as well. He asked God to withhold His judgment on the city if there were righteous men living there, beginning with fifty and working his way down to ten. It is tempting to wonder what the Lord might have said if Abraham had continued down to one righteous person, but we must not lose sight of what he was doing in this conversation. Abraham was interceding on behalf of people he didn't know—people, in fact, who were notoriously wicked and had caused him some personal hardship in the past. (See Genesis 14.) In addition, he was interceding for them with patience and diligence. In this, he is a role model for God's people of all generations.

25. FAR BE IT FROM YOU: Abraham was as concerned about the reputation of God as he was about the people of Sodom, suggesting that God's name would be smirched in the world if He were to act in an unjust manner toward those who serve Him.

SHALL NOT THE JUDGE OF ALL THE EARTH DO RIGHT?: Here again Abraham was trying to understand the character of God; he wanted to *know* God in the same intimate way that God knew him. His rhetorical question underscored the fact that God is inherently righteous and that He will of course always do what is just. Abraham was also keeping a right attitude about his own station in life, as he had in the entire conversation. He could easily have become puffed up, thinking himself more righteous than the people who lived in that wicked city. He could, on the other hand, have chosen to not worry about it, adopting a "let God be God" attitude and thinking no more about his neighbors. But instead, Abraham tried to imitate God in doing what was right, and this led him to intercede for his neighbors.

26. I WILL SPARE ALL THE PLACE FOR THEIR SAKES: Notice that this is above and beyond saving the righteous from the destruction of the wicked; this is imputing grace to the wicked on behalf of the righteous, thus sparing the wicked as well as the righteous. What we discover in this amazing offer of grace is that God's people can actually extend the grace of God to the world around them simply by their mere presence. This is part of what Jesus was referring to when He told His followers, "You are the salt of the earth" (Matthew 5:13). God's people are called to arrest corruption and bring healing, just as salt does—and as Lot failed to do.

27. I WHO AM BUT DUST AND ASHES: Abraham did not take his privilege for granted. God had reached out to him, permitting him the privilege of standing in His presence and speaking his mind freely, yet Abraham did not forget that he was but a sinful man in the presence of the Holy Creator. Jesus made it possible for Christians to "come boldly to the throne of grace" (Hebrews 4:16), yet we also do well to remember that we are but dust. We enter God's presence by His grace, not by our merit.

⌁ Reading James 2:17–23 ⌁

Faith without Works: *James addressed an important aspect of the Christian life, which he called "works." The works he spoke of are the many elements of a holy life that flow from a heart of faith.*

17. faith by itself: This passage must be balanced with Paul's teachings on the same topic in Romans 4. We will examine that passage in Study 10. James was making the point that it is faith—and faith alone—that saves us, but that saving faith will inevitably be followed by "works" of righteousness. In other words, our faith saves us and then flowers into righteous behavior.

18. your faith without your works: James was emphasizing the fact that our faith in Christ will always lead to holy living, loving our neighbors, serving others, considering others as better than ourselves, and the many other fruits of righteousness. A true saving faith will always lead to righteous works; you cannot have one without the other.

19. Even the demons believe: This is the difference between "believing" and "accepting." It is not enough to believe (in terms of mere intellectual assent) that Jesus is the Son of God and that He died on the cross and rose again in order to save us from our sins. We must also accept His free gift of salvation and affirm Him as our Lord and Savior; for even the demons believe the bare historical facts about Jesus, yet they are forever lost just the same.

Abraham's Example: *Abraham provides us with a good example of what James discussed here, because he had a faith that was carried out into works.*

21. justified by works when he offered Isaac his son on the altar: Abraham was declared righteous many years before Isaac was even born (see Genesis 15:6), as we saw in Study 2. What James meant here is that Abraham's saving faith—his righteousness in the eyes of God—was demonstrated to the world around him by his outward act of obedience when he sacrificed Isaac. As we saw in Study 4, God never sends a test that His children cannot pass, and He knew that Abraham's faith would impel him to obey God's command to sacrifice Isaac. He also knew that Abraham's saving faith would lead him to another element of "good works," as we saw in Genesis 18: interceding for others. All of these traits of Abraham are the good works that should result from our own faith in Jesus Christ.

22. BY WORKS FAITH WAS MADE PERFECT: This is what we see happening in Genesis 18 as Abraham interceded for the people of Sodom. God selected Abraham to be His representative to the world around him, to act as salt and light. Christians are called by God for the very same purpose. Having been saved by God's grace, we are subsequently called to show the grace of God *to* our neighbors. This calling is made complete, or "perfect," when our saving faith flowers and blooms into works of righteousness and love for the world around us.

23. ABRAHAM BELIEVED GOD: According to James, Genesis 15:6 was fulfilled on the day when Abraham offered his son Isaac on the altar. In other words, Abraham's faith saved him and brought him into righteousness before God, but this relationship was only "perfected" (tested and proven; brought to completion or fruition) when it led to good works in Abraham's life—from interceding for others to his willingness to sacrifice his beloved son.

THE FRIEND OF GOD: What an amazing title! And this is the very thing we saw in Genesis 18 as Abraham stood side by side with God, speaking to Him face-to-face as a man speaks to his friend. "No longer do I call you servants, for a servant does not know what his master is doing; but I have called you friends, for all things that I heard from My Father I have made known to you" (John 15:15).

⟿ First Impressions ⟿

1. *Abraham went to great lengths and risk to rescue Lot and the people of Sodom from captivity. (See Genesis 14.) How might you have responded if you were in his place in this passage?*

2. *Why do you think Abraham stopped when he got down to ten righteous people? Why not go all the way down to one? Would it have made any difference?*

3. What does this conversation reveal about Abraham's character?

4. What does this conversation reveal about God's character?

⤳ Some Key Principles ⤳

We are all called to be friends of God.

It is easy to become complacent about this concept, to take for granted what a price-less treasure we have in our relationship with God through Christ. When we pray, we are entering freely into the very presence of the Creator of the universe! This is a privilege that came at tremendous cost—the painful death of God's own Son—and we Christians can easily forget how privileged we are.

As God's friends, we are invited to enter His presence at any time—more than this, we are urged to do so, as God is actually eager to fellowship with us! Abraham demon-strated the proper attitude toward this incredible blessing when he stood with God to speak as a man speaks to a friend—and then stepped even closer to speak to Him inti-mately. This attitude is both pleasing to God and profitable to His children.

Friendship is a two-way relationship.

God made Abraham His friend, and He came to his home for an unexpected visit. Abraham did nothing to initiate that visit, but he did respond by welcoming the Lord and His angels with a costly feast. He did not initiate the conversation with God as the angels departed for Sodom, but he did respond by deliberately drawing closer and speak-ing intimately with his Creator.

We do nothing to initiate or accomplish our salvation, but we can do much to in-crease our intimacy with God. He already knows us intimately—better than we know ourselves and even to the point of numbering the hairs on our heads. He also wants us to know Him intimately, and this is the point where our fellowship with Him requires effort from us.

We come to know God intimately when we follow the examples of men such as Abraham, David, and other saints from Scripture. Deliberately drawing close to Him in worship, interceding for others, confessing our sins promptly and fully, studying His Word to learn more about His character—these are just a few of the things that God's friends will do to deepen their friendship with Him.

We are saved by faith, but our faith must be demonstrated by good works.

This is a difficult concept to grasp. There is always the danger that we will become proud of our works and think that we are saved because we are special, or we may fall into legalism and believe that we must add to God's salvation by our own works. Neither of these extremes is true, yet we are still called to show forth our salvation by the works of our lives.

Abraham was found righteous in God's eyes when he believed God's promise—believing it despite the fact that it was utterly impossible for him to have children. This same faith in God's promise, in God's character, led him later to believe that God could raise Isaac from the dead, and this led him to act in faith by being willing to sacrifice his son. In this way, his faith was producing both his salvation *and* his good works, and it was by both together that his faith was proven to the world around him.

When we obey God's Word and live holy lives, the world around us will see the reality of our faith. Words alone cannot accomplish this. When we preach our faith but don't *live* by faith, we are acting no better than the devil's minions—they, too, know God's truth, but their empty belief is insufficient to save them. When we accept Christ as our Savior, we also receive the Holy Spirit into our lives, and He is faithful to produce the fruit of our salvation for all to see.

∼ DIGGING DEEPER ∼

5. *What does it mean to be a friend of God? What does it mean to be friends with the world? Give practical examples of each.*

6. What things did God do to demonstrate His friendship with Abraham in this passage and others? What did Abraham do to deepen that friendship?

7. What does it mean to love your neighbor? How does a Christian draw a line between loving a sinner and condoning sin?

8. What is the difference between being saved by faith and saved by good works? How do good works play a part in a Christian's life?

↳ Taking It Personally ↰

9. What are you doing to deepen your friendship with God? What could you do that you aren't doing now?

10. Start a prayer list for people in your life—family, friends, neighbors, co-workers, etc. Pray for those people regularly, and let them know you are praying for them.

7
SARAH

∽ CHARACTER'S BACKGROUND ∽

We have been looking quite a bit at the life and person of Abraham, but in the process we must not overlook another important character in the history of God's chosen people: his wife Sarah. She was Abraham's half sister, sharing the same father but having different mothers. In Abraham's day, such marriages were not uncommon.

Sarah appears in the background of many of the passages we have been considering, yet her presence is still very real. She was evidently very beautiful—even into her old age; she possessed the sort of beauty that could catch the eye of a king. She was chosen by God to be the mother of Isaac, God's promised son in the line of Jesus Himself. She is to be found inside her husband's tent, preparing a feast at the spur of the moment for unexpected guests. On a less proud occasion, she persuaded her husband to stop waiting for God to fulfill His promise and take matters into their own hands.

She was a woman who, like her husband, was a very real human being. Scripture records her foibles and failures just as much as her victories and joy. She was far from perfect, yet the New Testament points to her as a woman of great character, worthy of our emulation today. It may come as a surprise in our modern day of "liberated women" to discover that she never headed up a corporation or ran for president. In fact, Peter points to her as an example of godly womanhood specifically because of her quiet and gentle spirit—and her behind-the-scenes role in the life of her husband.

In this study, we will take a closer look at this great woman and consider what made her so special. What can modern Christians learn from the life of Sarah, a woman who was significant in the line of Christ?

SARAH LAUGHS: *The Lord came to visit Abraham on His way to judge Sodom and Gomorrah, and He promised a child within the year. But Sarah laughed.*

9. THEY SAID TO HIM: The Lord and two of His angels had come to visit Abraham in Mamre, prior to the destruction of Sodom. Abraham was seated outside of his tent, while Sarah was inside.

10. ACCORDING TO THE TIME OF LIFE: The Lord was promising that Abraham and Sarah would give birth to their promised son, Isaac, within the coming year—and He kept His promise.

11. ABRAHAM AND SARAH WERE OLD: Sarah was around age ninety, Abraham around one hundred.

SARAH HAD PASSED THE AGE OF CHILDBEARING: This was precisely the Lord's intention in His promises to Abraham concerning an heir. He allowed the couple to get well beyond the point where it was physically possible for them to bear children, because he wanted the birth of Isaac to be an undeniable miracle. This would be a foreshadowing of the miraculous virgin birth of Jesus Himself. The Lord also wanted to stretch the faith of both Abraham and Sarah in this process, teaching them that "with God all things are possible" (Mark 10:27).

12. SARAH LAUGHED: We can hardly blame Sarah for this laughter. If someone told a ninety-year-old woman today that she was going to have a baby within a year, laughter might be among the most gentle of responses that one could expect. Abraham himself had laughed not long before when the Lord appeared to him. (See Genesis 17:17.)

WITHIN HERSELF: That is, she did not laugh aloud.

HE KNOWS OUR THOUGHTS: *Sarah was sitting inside the tent, and the Lord and His angels were outside. They could not see her, and she had not spoken. Yet the Lord knew her thoughts.*

13. WHY DID SARAH LAUGH?: The Lord knows even our most intimate thoughts (see Psalm 94:11), but this must have been disconcerting for Sarah as she sat inside the tent, out of view of the strange men who were outside. The Lord went beyond her laughter and even quoted the very thoughts of her mind; it is no wonder that she became frightened.

14. IS ANYTHING TOO HARD FOR THE LORD?: This is at the core of this difficult lesson for Sarah and Abraham, and the Lord insisted that they both learn the lesson fully. It is an important lesson for all God's children, but it was also important in the prophecies concerning the Messiah, whose birth would be the most miraculous, impossible human birth of all time. Compared with Jesus' virgin birth, Isaac's birth was a piece of cake.

15. I DID NOT LAUGH: It is quite understandable that Sarah was frightened at this point. This Man who was speaking outside the tent to her husband was clearly more than a mere mortal. Yet she was still not justified in lying—even though it was technically only a "half lie": Sarah had laughed *inwardly*, not literally out loud. But God does not countenance lies in any form, not even when they are half true. This was the same problem that Abraham had—more than once—in telling people that Sarah was his sister but not his wife.

SHE WAS AFRAID: Sarah and Abraham would each be required to learn to trust God, having a holy "fear" that is reverential awe, but which is quite devoid of fearful anxiety.

(1-32)

⤳ READING GENESIS 21:1–8 ⤳

MIRACLE BIRTH: *Within a year, Sarah gave birth to Isaac—just as the Lord had promised. It had taken some twenty-five years, but at last the Lord's promise had come to pass.*

3. ISAAC: Literally, "he laughs." God had directed Abraham to bestow this name on his son after Abraham laughed in disbelief at God's promise. (See Genesis 17:19.) The name became doubly appropriate when Sarah laughed in the same manner. The name, however, would commemorate a more joyful laughter rather than these brief episodes of doubt on the part of the boy's parents.

4. ABRAHAM CIRCUMCISED HIS SON ISAAC: See Genesis 17. This rite of circumcision was immensely important prior to the time of Christ, because it was the outward display of a man's commitment to Jehovah. This ties together with what we considered in Study 6—the combination of faith and works in the life of a Christian. Circumcision was the outward display of one's faith, even as obedience and good works are the outward display of a Christian's faith.

5. ABRAHAM WAS ONE HUNDRED YEARS OLD: Sarah was ninety.

SON OF LAUGHTER: *And now, at last, Sarah's faith was rewarded, her righteousness made evident to the world around her—and her laughter made joyful.*

6. GOD HAS MADE ME LAUGH: Sarah's derisive, mocking laughter had been turned to joy, making the name Isaac ("he laughs") all the more appropriate. "Sing, O barren, you who have not borne! Break forth into singing, and cry aloud, you who have not labored with child! For more are the children of the desolate than the children of the married woman" (Isaiah 54:1).

ALL WHO HEAR: This brings us back to the basic reason that God chose Abraham and Sarah for this purpose: they were to be beacons to the world around them, demonstrating God's grace and showing the nations what it meant to be a follower of Jehovah. Sarah realized that the world was watching, and in this glorious moment her faith was vindicated.

7. WHO WOULD HAVE SAID TO ABRAHAM THAT SARAH WOULD NURSE CHILDREN?: Sarah was expressing her unmixed wonder at God's miraculous fulfillment, a birth (and subsequent nursing) that were physically impossible. Yet her words also incriminated her to a degree—for the simple reason that God Himself had told Abraham that Sarah would nurse children! God's Word always comes to pass, and He never fails to keep His promises. Never.

8. WEANED: This usually occurred in the second or third year.

⌒ READING 1 PETER 3:1–12 ⌒

BE SUBMISSIVE: *Peter discussed the Christian's calling to be submissive in the previous chapter, and here he turned his attention to husbands and wives.*

1. LIKEWISE: In the previous chapter, Peter expounded on the fact that Christians are called to be submissive to Christ and to one another. Now he carries this doctrine into the home, urging wives to submit to the spiritual leadership of their husbands and husbands to show honor to their wives.

BE SUBMISSIVE TO YOUR OWN HUSBANDS: This doctrine goes across the grain in modern Western society, but Christians are called upon to obey the Word of God, not the teachings of the world around us. The Greek word translated *submissive* is a compound word, meaning to "rank under." It means that the wife should voluntarily consider herself to be under the rank, or authority, of her husband—to consider him as outranking her. Notice also how Peter qualified this: "submissive to your *own* husbands." This underscores the fact that a woman is not inferior to a man any more than one Christian is inferior to another. He was addressing roles within *marriage* and calling the wife to consider herself as "outranked" by her husband—but not by other men.

EVEN IF SOME DO NOT OBEY THE WORD: This teaching applies to wives whose husbands are not Christians, as well as those whose husbands obey the Word of God. This hierarchy of authority goes back to Creation, before mankind even fell into sin.

A Quiet Witness: *A Christian woman can actually lead her unsaved husband to Christ—without speaking a word. This is done by submission.*

THAT . . . THEY . . . MAY BE WON BY THE CONDUCT OF THEIR WIVES: Here Peter gives one reason for this teaching: a submissive Christian wife may impel her unbelieving husband toward Christ by the simple example of her obedience to God's Word. This is accomplished "without a word," Peter says, because actions speak louder than words. A wife's example of submission to her husband is an example of being submissive to Christ, and this example alone—without any unnecessary preaching—is enough to demonstrate the reality of her faith. The loving, gracious submission of a Christian woman to her unsaved husband is the strongest evangelistic tool she has.

2. WHEN THEY OBSERVE: The word translated "observe" means "to view attentively." Peter was suggesting that the unsaved husband would be watching his wife closely to see how well she lived out her faith—and how well her faith worked in her life. This ties back to Sarah's comment, "God has made me laugh, and all who hear will laugh with me" (Genesis 21:6).

CHASTE CONDUCT ACCOMPANIED BY FEAR: Fear in the sense of reverence—both toward God and toward her husband.

Hidden Person of the Heart: *We are not to spend time worrying about our outward appearance; it is the inner person that matters.*

3. DO NOT LET YOUR ADORNMENT BE MERELY OUTWARD: Paul was not condemning outward adornments or a woman's desire to make herself presentable or even stylish. He was warning against allowing that to become a preoccupation or obsession—a danger that is very real in our modern culture. A Christian's focus should be on the inner person, not the outer appearance—and this doctrine applies just as much to men as to women.

4. THE HIDDEN PERSON OF THE HEART: The word *hidden* comes from *cryptos*, from which we get our English words *cryptic* and *encryption*. It implies a secret, such as the encryption that is used to keep computer data from being stolen. The hidden person of the heart is the deepest, secret, inner person—the "real you" that only God can fully know.

INCORRUPTIBLE BEAUTY: A woman's beauty will generally fade as she ages, but a godly woman's inner beauty will increase as she grows in the likeness of Christ. Once again, this ties back to Sarah, in the sense that her body had aged beyond the ability to produce or nurse a baby, but God miraculously brought forth a deeper, more lasting beauty in her old age.

GENTLE AND QUIET SPIRIT: The gentleness refers to meekness and humility, a gentleness of spirit. The quiet spirit is one that is not easily ruffled—either by circumstances or by a husband who is difficult to get along with. These qualities are "very precious in the sight of God."

SARAH'S EXAMPLE: *Peter turned to Sarah as the example of a godly, submissive wife.*

---

6. CALLING HIM LORD: It is interesting that Peter should point to this instance in Genesis 18:12, since Sarah was actually voicing her doubts as to whether God could keep His promise. Yet the Lord remembered her faith, not her doubts. It can be difficult at times to cling to our trust of God's Word when circumstances go against us, and this can certainly be true for a woman's submission to an ungodly husband. But the Lord strengthens our doubts, building our faith each time we act in faith and obedience.

WHOSE DAUGHTERS YOU ARE: We become sons of Abraham and daughters of Sarah when we act in faith and obey God's Word.

NOT AFRAID WITH ANY TERROR: We have seen numerous times in Abraham's life where fear led him away from God rather than toward faith. See, for example, Study 1. There are potential fears for a Christian woman who sets out to be submissive to her unsaved husband, such as whether that submission will lead toward God's will or away from it. Peter's injunction to submit to an ungodly husband, however, does not include any coercion to sin or disobey God's Word; nor does it require physical harm (compare Acts 5:28–29).

HUSBANDS: *Men are called upon to submit to their wives—in fact, they are called to the more difficult task of loving their wives as Christ loved the church.*

---

7. HUSBANDS, LIKEWISE: Husbands are also called to be humble and submissive (see Ephesians 5:21), although the role of submission is different from that of the wife. The husband is the spiritual head of the home, yet he is to lead by example rather than by tyranny. A man who desires a loving, gentle wife must demonstrate how to be loving and gentle himself.

UNDERSTANDING: This word in the Greek is *gnosis*, meaning knowledge. A cult arose in the early church (which has resurfaced in modern times under the guise of science) that taught that a person needed some "higher knowledge" if he was to fully understand God's Word. Yet here Peter touched upon the *true* higher knowledge to which every Christian is called: the knowledge of love and patience toward others. A godly husband must submit himself to the task of learning to love and understand his wife, deliberately subordinating his needs to hers—whether she is a Christian or not. Peter specifically noted consideration, chivalry, and companionship.

HONOR: Showing deference and reverence.

HEIRS TOGETHER OF THE GRACE OF LIFE: Man and woman together complete the image of God. (See Genesis 1:27.) The "grace of life" here is not salvation but marriage. The husband must cultivate companionship and fellowship with his wife.

THAT YOUR PRAYERS MAY NOT BE HINDERED: A Christian man must love his wife as Christ loved the church (see Ephesians 5:25), setting her needs above his own. If he does not, Peter warned, his very prayers will be hindered. (See Matthew 5:23–24.)

⌁ FIRST IMPRESSIONS ⌁

1. *How would you respond at age ninety if someone told you that you would have a baby within the year?*

2. *How would you have reacted if a stranger arrived for dinner and began to tell you what you were thinking? What does this reveal about God's feelings toward Sarah?*

3. *How does Sarah's faith in God's promises compare with Abraham's faith?*

4. *In what ways does the birth of Isaac prefigure the birth of Christ?*

﹏ Some Key Principles ﹏

Nothing is impossible for God.

Imagine how Sarah must have felt, even at age sixty-five when God first appeared to Abraham, to hear that God was going to give her a child. Imagine further how she must have felt when twenty-five years went past without any pregnancy. Now imagine how Mary must have felt when an angel told her that she was already pregnant—and she was still a virgin!

The Lord deliberately waited until it was painfully clear that a birth was impossible, both for Sarah and for Mary. And then He gave them sons! This was done, in part, to prove beyond any doubt that the children were miracles of God and that no man could lay any claim to having engineered that miracle.

God still calls His children to exercise total faith in Him and the promises of His Word—no matter how difficult the circumstances may seem. Perhaps He has asked you to do something that seems impossible—remain with an unsaved spouse, for example—and you just can't see how He can ever work it for His glory. But nothing is impossible for God, and He is always faithful to His promises and to His children. When He asks us to do the impossible, our job is to obey and then trust Him with the outcome. Those who put their faith and hope in God will not be disappointed.

The man is the head of the Christ-centered home.

This teaching is hard for many in the church, because our modern feminist culture spurns the concept of "gender roles." Feminists would shriek in disdain if told that a husband "outranks" the wife in the spiritual leadership of the home—yet this is precisely what Peter (and other biblical writers) would have us accept.

This teaching can be even more frightening for a Christian who is married to an unbeliever. It is no accident that Peter addressed both of these topics in the same passage; he made it clear that a wife's submission to her husband applies whether the husband is a Christian or not.

The reason for this is that when a woman submits herself to her husband's headship, she is indirectly submitting herself to Christ's headship. Even if that husband is not a believer, the wife will bring honor to God by submitting to the divinely ordained structure of authority for the home. There is no safer or better place for anyone to be than in direct submission to Christ.

God's people must submit to one another.

This principle is closely related to the previous one and applies throughout the church, regardless of one believer's relationship to another. But once again, it is a teaching that is unpopular in our culture, which teaches that "submission" is essentially the same as slavery. This is the opposite of what Scripture teaches; God's Word makes it clear that a Christian can never know true freedom in Christ until he or she has learned to humbly serve others.

Paul addressed this same issue regarding wives submitting to their husbands, but he prefaced that passage with the admonition that God's people should be "submitting to one another in the fear of God" (Ephesians 5:21). Elsewhere he tells us, "Let nothing be done through selfish ambition or conceit, but in lowliness of mind let each esteem others better than himself. Let each of you look out not only for his own interests, but also for the interests of others" (Philippians 2:3–4).

Submission actually has little to do with authority and everything to do with godliness. It is a voluntary act, a deliberate decision to put someone else's needs before our own. In making this decision, we are becoming imitators of Christ.

⌁ DIGGING DEEPER ⌁

5. *Why do you think God confronted Sarah when she laughed and had doubting thoughts? What did this confrontation show about God's character? What did Sarah learn?*

6. *Abraham and Sarah had real doubts about God's promise, and they even committed serious sin out of that doubt. Why did God still fulfill the promise? What does this show about His character? About His promises?*

7. Why did the Lord take so long to fulfill His promise of a son for Abraham and Sarah? Why did He wait until pregnancy and child rearing were so utterly impossible by human standards?

8. Why does God expect a woman to submit to her husband's authority? How does this teaching correspond with society's views?

⤙ TAKING IT PERSONALLY ⤚

9. How do you feel about the teachings concerning a woman's submission to her husband? If you are married, how does your marriage address this? If single, what sort of marriage do you desire?

10. What does Sarah's life teach us about trusting in God and His promises? How will her example help you the next time you encounter a situation that you believe to be impossible?

8

ISAAC

GENESIS 16, 21, 22; GALATIANS 4

⮌ CHARACTER'S BACKGROUND ⮌

In order to appreciate Isaac more fully, it will be helpful if we also look at his half brother, Ishmael. We must, therefore, return once more to the time before Isaac's birth, when Abraham and Sarah were still called Abram and Sarai.

We have seen that Isaac was the "son of promise," the heir that God had promised to Abraham many times over. God had told Abraham repeatedly that he would become a great nation and that his descendants would be so numerable that no man could hope to count them—like the sand on the seashore. God had also made it quite clear that this promise would come through a son of miraculous birth, a child born through the union of Abram and his wife, Sarai.

But God had promised this many times over a period of at least ten years, and ten years is a very long time to wait for a promised son to be born—especially when you are seventy-five years old to begin with! It would be a miracle if a woman in her late seventies gave birth to a child, especially if her husband were in his mid-eighties.

So it is not surprising to find that Sarai was beginning to have doubts about God's promise. To make matters worse, she and her husband began to *act* on their doubts, rather than on their faith. As a result, they found themselves falling into sin and making very bad decisions. They decided to take matters into their own hands, and the consequences are still with us today.

Sarai's scheme did lead to a birth, as her handmaid Hagar bore Abram a son named Ishmael. But God rejected Ishmael as the son of promise and made it very clear that Ishmael could not share in Isaac's inheritance. As we will see in this study, Paul used these two young men to illustrate another truth of Scripture: man's works cannot play any part in God's plan of salvation, for we are saved by grace alone. (See Study 6 for the flip side to this issue.)

⤳ READING GENESIS 16:1–6 ⤷

WRESTLING WITH DOUBT: *Abram and Sarai are still waiting for the appearance of Isaac, and it's been at least ten years since God promised a son. They decide that maybe they should help God along.*

1. SARAI, ABRAM'S WIFE: We have gone back to the time prior to Abram's circumcision, when he received the new name of Abraham. This is an important distinction to understand, since the circumcision marked a new relationship between God and Abraham. The circumcision represented a sort of "rebirth" in which Abram received his new name. This distinction will become more important as we move into our New Testament passages.

HAD BORNE HIM NO CHILDREN: God had promised Abram repeatedly that he would have a son and countless descendants, but that son would not arrive until after Abram had been circumcised, cutting off the flesh. This was part of God's picture of the final redemption plan when we are reborn into the family of Christ.

AN EGYPTIAN MAIDSERVANT: As we saw in Study 1, the nation of Egypt is frequently used in Scripture to represent the world's system. There is a good possibility that Hagar was one of the servants that Pharaoh gave to Abram during his sojourn there when Abram was trying to escape a famine in Canaan. (See Study 1 for more information.)

2. THE LORD HAS RESTRAINED ME: This statement was technically true, for the Lord is the giver of life. Yet it reflected a lack of faith in Sarai's thinking; she was growing impatient waiting for the Lord to fulfill His promise. There may even be a degree of resentment in her words, as though she was blaming God for her childlessness.

I SHALL OBTAIN: Sarai's focus was on herself and her own plans and dreams more than on the larger picture. God had promised more than a son for Abram and Sarai: He had promised an entire nation, descendants that could not be numbered. And, in the bigger picture still, He had promised a Redeemer, the Seed who would one day save mankind from sin. God's plan certainly included the personal longings of Abram and Sarai for a son, yet it was far, far bigger than that. The results of Sarai's scheme would also last far longer than she anticipated.

CHILDREN BY HER: God had told Abram, "One who will come from your own body shall be your heir" (Genesis 15:4). Technically, the son born through Hagar would be from Abram's own body, but the Lord meant that the heir would be born through his proper union with his own wife, Sarai. The Lord had decreed in the garden of Eden that a man would "be joined to his wife, and they shall become one flesh" (Genesis 2:24), and Abram would have understood this from the Lord's promise.

Sarai Takes Charge: *Sarai cooked up a plan of her own to assist God in the business of producing an heir. Hagar was probably a gift from Pharaoh when they were in Egypt.*

Abram heeded the voice of Sarai: Abram repeated the sin of Adam by placing himself under the spiritual authority of his wife. (See Genesis 3:17.) The Lord had just recently come to Abram in a vision and made a formal covenant with him, which is recorded in Genesis 15. God had bolstered Abram's faith and encouraged him, but then he turned right around and allowed his wife to take the lead.

3. Sarai, Abram's wife, took Hagar her maid: Sarai took the leadership of the situation, and Abram submitted to her headship, just as Adam and Eve did. Eve perceived a problem that didn't exist, thanks to the direct lies of the serpent, and she took matters into her own hands to resolve that nonexistent problem. Sarai perceived that there was a problem with God's promise being fulfilled, so she took matters into her own hands to resolve it. The results in both cases were immensely disastrous, affecting all of mankind for all time. (The son born through Hagar led to the Arabic nations, which are still at war with Israel even today.)

4. her mistress became despised: This was just the beginning of woes from this bad plan.

5. My wrong be upon you: This, of course, was grossly unfair, since the entire plan was Sarai's in the first place. Yet it is also quite literally true, for the Lord would hold Abram responsible for abdicating his spiritual authority in the home, just as He held Adam responsible in Eden. (See Genesis 3:17.)

⌁ Reading Genesis 21:8–14 ⌁

Mocking the Heir: *Ishmael was probably about fifteen years older than Isaac, approximately seventeen at the time Isaac was weaned. He was not a gracious older brother.*

8. weaned: Isaac was probably around two or three at this time.

9. the son of Hagar: Ishmael.

10. shall not be heir with my son: This was what God told Abraham in the first place. (See Genesis 15:3–4; 17:18–20.) Sarah's plan accomplished nothing good—as the couple found themselves back where they had been in the first place—but it did accomplish much that was not good.

11. THE MATTER WAS VERY DISPLEASING IN ABRAHAM'S SIGHT: In other words, this time Abraham refused to heed his wife's counsel.

12. LISTEN TO HER VOICE: This time Abraham sought the Lord's will and discovered (ironically) that his wife's advice was in accordance with God's plan. The difference, however, lay in the fact that Abraham sought God's will and took his proper role as spiritual head of the household.

13. I WILL ALSO MAKE A NATION OF THE SON OF THE BONDWOMAN: Ishmael's descendants include many of the modern Arabic nations. There has always been grievous enmity between them and Israel, and the descendants of Isaac have suffered greatly from the descendants of Ishmael.

14. SENT HER AWAY: This seems horribly heartless, yet we must remember that this situation would never have arisen in the first place if Abraham had not tried to take matters into his own hands with Hagar. God had made it abundantly clear that His promise would be fulfilled through Isaac alone and that He would not tolerate any adulteration of His chosen seed. As we will see in the New Testament, it was essential that Ishmael be sent away from Isaac, for Isaac alone was the chosen heir of Abraham, and he could not share that inheritance.

ᴄ READING GENESIS 22:6–9 ᴄ

ISAAC, PICTURE OF CHRIST: *We now move ahead to when Isaac was a young man in his late teens or early twenties. His attitude and actions made a powerful picture of the Messiah who was to come.*

6. LAID IT ON ISAAC: Isaac presented an excellent picture of the Lord Jesus as He voluntarily went to the cross to provide the final sacrifice for sins. Isaac carried the wood that was to be his own funeral pyre, just as Jesus carried His cross to Calvary.

THE TWO OF THEM WENT TOGETHER: Isaac was not a little boy; he was at least fourteen years old and probably older. He most likely had at least a suspicion of what his father had in mind and may well have divined his intentions fairly thoroughly, as we'll see in the next verse. Yet he made no struggle at all and walked together with his father in complete unity. Here again we see a picture of the person of Jesus, God's only begotten Son, who walked in perfect unity with the Father all the way to the cross.

7. WHERE IS THE LAMB: We are not told how much Isaac knew of his father's intentions, but it would appear that Abraham had told him little if anything. In this, Isaac differs from the Lord Jesus, who was fully aware of what His Father's purpose was in sending Him into the world. Yet even Isaac in this passage appeared to have a glimmer of what was coming, and like Christ, he made no complaint.

8. THE TWO OF THEM WENT TOGETHER: It is interesting that this phrase is repeated here. Ancient Jewish writers claim that Isaac by this time knew that he was to be sacrificed—and that he was willing to trust his father in the matter. There is no question that before the ordeal was over, Isaac knew full well what was happening. Once again, he typified Christ in his absolute dedication to be like-minded with his father.

9. HE BOUND ISAAC: Picture this scene in your mind, as a man who is at least 115 years old attempts to tie up a youth in his late teens or early twenties. Isaac could at the very least have resisted his father and probably could easily have overpowered him. Yet he was completely docile—even cooperative. By this time it was abundantly evident that Abraham intended to slay his son and burn his body on the altar—yet Isaac cooperated fully.

⌁ READING GALATIANS 3:29–4:5 ⌁

ABRAHAM'S HEIRS: *Paul teaches us that Christians are adopted into the family of God and that we inherit all the blessings that He gave to Abraham.*

3:29. YOU ARE ABRAHAM'S SEED: When we accept Jesus as our Lord and Savior, we become adopted into the family of God. We are spiritual descendants of Abraham in the sense that we follow the pattern of his faith and are heir to all the promises of God.

4:1. THE HEIR: Paul used Isaac and Ishmael in a symbolic way to represent grace and legalism, respectively.

4. BORN UNDER THE LAW: Paul was referring to the law of Moses, which God gave to the Israelites during their exodus from Egypt. The Old Testament law consisted of many animal sacrifices and other stipulations that God required of His people if they were to remain in fellowship with Him. Jesus was literally "born under the law" in the sense that the law of Moses was still in effect when He was born. But after His death and resurrection, that law was abolished.

⌁ READING GALATIANS 4:21–31 ⌁

ISAAC AND ISHMAEL AS SYMBOLS: *Paul used these two young men to illustrate the fact that Christians are under grace, set free from the law of Moses.*

22. TWO SONS: Ishmael and Isaac, respectively.

23. BORN ACCORDING TO THE FLESH: As we have seen, Ishmael was born because Sarai and Abram tried to take God's will into their own hands. He thus represents legalism in Paul's letter, since legalism is man's attempt to earn righteousness apart from God's grace.

24. SYMBOLIC: That is, Paul was using Isaac and Ishmael as symbolic examples of doctrine. He was not suggesting that they were not literal, historical people.

THE TWO COVENANTS: The first covenant was the law of Moses, given at Mount Sinai during Israel's exodus from Egypt. The second covenant was one of grace, given on Mount Calvary when Christ died for our sins.

GIVES BIRTH TO BONDAGE: The law of Moses brought bondage to the people of Israel in the sense that they had an endless array of works to perform in order to obtain forgiveness for sins. This presents the other side of what we discussed in Study 6, where we saw that good works are the natural outgrowth of saving faith. Here we see that good works are utterly powerless to save us from sin; we are saved by grace alone.

25. HAGAR IS MOUNT SINAI: That is, Hagar symbolically represents the law of Moses, which was given to Israel on Mount Sinai.

IS IN BONDAGE WITH HER CHILDREN: It is significant that God told Abraham to send away Hagar and Ishmael. Hagar was a bondwoman, an indentured servant who did not have the inherent rights that Abraham's wife, Sarah, had. Her son also was a bondservant, with no inherent rights of a natural son. God told Abraham to send them away because He would not allow anyone but Isaac to enjoy Abraham's inheritance. Paul applied this teaching to the conflict between grace and legalism, showing that mankind's good works do not and cannot play a part—not even the smallest part—in our salvation. "For by grace you have been saved through faith, and that not of yourselves; it is the gift of God, not of works, lest anyone should boast" (Ephesians 2:8–9).

26. THE JERUSALEM ABOVE: Paul was referring to the eternal kingdom of God. "By faith Abraham obeyed when he was called to go out to the place which he would receive as an inheritance. And he went out, not knowing where he was going. By faith he dwelt in the land of promise as in a foreign country, dwelling in tents with Isaac and Jacob, the heirs with him of the same promise; for he waited for the city which has foundations, whose builder and maker is God" (Hebrews 11:8–10).

29. PERSECUTED HIM: The flesh and spirit are always at war within a Christian, just as Ishmael persecuted Isaac—a war that continues, quite literally, even in modern times. Similarly, the law of Moses cannot work together with the grace of God to bring about our salvation. Legalism only takes Christians back into bondage and is constantly at war with the Spirit.

➳ First Impressions ➳

1. If you had been in Sarai's place, how would you have felt about God's promises for a son? Would you have tried to give God some help?

2. Why did Sarah insist that Hagar and Ishmael be sent away? Why did God command Abraham to do so?

3. Put yourself in Ishmael's place. Why might he have persecuted Isaac, who was only an infant?

4. How would you have felt if you had been in Isaac's place, going up the mountain to be sacrificed? What do we learn about Jesus from Isaac's example?

↤ Some Key Principles ↦

Christians are called to do good works, but our good works can never save us.

This is the flip side to the principle that we looked at in Study 6. It is important that we examine both sides of this principle, because both are vital to our lives as Christians.

We are saved by faith, and faith alone, through the grace of God. By "saved," we mean that our sins have been permanently forgiven, once and for all, and we have been brought into an eternal relationship with God because Jesus paid the price for our sins on the cross. This salvation could not have been accomplished by any human being who has ever walked this planet, with one exception, simply because every human who has ever lived has been a sinner—and a sinner cannot pay for someone else's sins, nor for his own. The only Person who could accomplish this was the one Person who lived a sinless life: Jesus.

God is faithful to apply Jesus' payment to our sin-debt when we repent of our sins and ask Him for forgiveness. This step of repentance is accomplished by faith, and there is nothing whatsoever that any person can ever do to accomplish it except to receive it in faith.

It is not a sin to have questions about what God is doing, but acting out of doubt will lead to sin.

As we have seen in previous studies, God sometimes asks us to trust Him to accomplish the impossible. We are only made of dust, and it is natural to have doubts at times as to how God will fulfill His promises.

The problem is not in having occasional doubts or questions, but in *acting* on them out of fear or frustration. Sarai and Abram had the choice between acting on their doubts and acting on their faith. Acting on faith would have meant doing essentially nothing, apart from maintaining normal marital relations. The difficult aspect of that, however, is the very fact of *doing nothing*. There are times when the most difficult course of action is *no* action at all—to wait patiently on God's timing.

Yet that is precisely the course that Abram and Sarai should have followed, patiently continuing to wait for God's own timetable. Instead, they focused on their doubts, persuaded themselves that God's promise could not be fulfilled without their help, and took matters into their own hands. That particular sin had consequences that will exist until the end of time.

We can never predict the consequences of sin.

Sarai probably did not think that her plan concerning Hagar was sinful, and she certainly never thought that it would bring about suffering for her own family. Abram may well have understood that Sarai's plan was sinful, yet he did not stop to count the cost of disobedience.

There are times when we persuade ourselves that "this one little bit" of sinful behavior won't hurt, "just this once." But Abram's single act of disobedience with Hagar led to countless deaths and acts of persecution, which have continued for several thousand years. Consider what a small sin Adam committed when he merely ate a piece of fruit.

Humans are specialists at self-deception and self-justification. We can always excuse and condone the "little sins" that we commit. But we should keep in mind that we cannot predict what consequences each "one little sin" may produce—how many innocent people may suffer, how long the ripples may continue, or even what price we may pay ourselves.

⌒ DIGGING DEEPER ⌒

5. *What sorts of "help" might have been legitimate for Abram and Sarai to give in fulfilling God's promises? What made Sarai's plan not legitimate?*

6. *Why do you think Abram consented to Sarai's plan if he understood it was wrong? How might he have justified it in his own mind?*

7. In view of Paul's discussion of grace versus the law, why were Hagar and Ishmael (symbolic of the law) sent away from Isaac (symbolic of grace)?

8. Why did Paul use Isaac and Ishmael as symbols of grace and legalism? How does this symbolism help you understand these concepts?

↼ Taking It Personally ↽

9. What doubts are you struggling with? What course of action does the Lord want you to take?

10. Do you understand the distinction between "good works" (loving, grace-filled obedience) and "legalism"? Which of these does your life reflect?

9

JACOB

GENESIS 28, 29

⤳ CHARACTER'S BACKGROUND ⤶

We saw in Study 5 how Jacob stole his brother's birthright by guile. Esau was very angry, understandably, and vowed to kill Jacob, so his parents sent Jacob off to live with his mother's brother Laban for a time. Our passage opens with Jacob heading off to his uncle's—but he had an unexpected meeting with God along the way.

He eventually arrived at his uncle Laban's home and spent many years working there, tending sheep and livestock for his uncle. During those years he also married Laban's two daughters, Leah and Rachel. He also managed to become very wealthy by using some rather devious tricks to enrich himself from his father-in-law's flocks.

But Jacob was also on the receiving end of crafty guile during this time. He fell in love with Rachel, Laban's younger daughter, and agreed to work for seven years to attain her hand in marriage. But when the wedding day arrived, Uncle Laban treacherously substituted older sister Leah instead of Jacob's beloved Rachel. Jacob was forced to work for another seven years to gain the hand of Rachel as his second wife.

Tensions and distrust also began to breed within Jacob's family. He demonstrated love toward Rachel, while making poor Leah feel unloved and unwanted—so God consoled her with many children, while Rachel remained barren. This, needless to say, created further tension and resentment within the home, and Jacob bore the brunt of the bitterness and heartache of his two wives—and several concubines for good measure.

After many years, when Jacob was nearly one hundred years old, he found himself forced to leave his uncle's household. Family friction and suspicion had increased to the point where the two men could no longer live together, so Jacob headed back toward Bethel, where he had met God many years before. Unfortunately, his brother Esau learned of his arrival and rode out to meet him—with four hundred men in his company! Jacob found himself caught between two men whom he had swindled, and in desperation he finally called upon the name of the Lord.

Jacob's treachery and deceit were coming back to torment him, but God had a great blessing in store as well.

JACOB'S DREAM: *Esau had vowed to kill Jacob for his treachery, so his parents sent him off to live with his uncle Laban. Along the way, he stopped for the night.*

11. A CERTAIN PLACE: Haran. (See map in the Introduction.)

12. A LADDER: This dream offers a graphic portrayal of the Lord's personal involvement in the affairs of the earth, and here especially as they related to divine covenant promises in Jacob's life. (See Genesis 28:13–15.) This dream was to encourage the lonely traveler. God's own appointed angelic messengers carried out His will and plans. More than likely, the angels traversed a stairway rather than a ladder.

13–15. I WILL GIVE TO YOU: God now repeated for Jacob the same promises He had given to Abraham: he would inherit the land, his descendants would be innumerable, and his descendants would become a blessing to the nations. The Lord also revealed a new detail that we have not encountered before: Jacob's descendants would also "spread abroad to the west and the east, to the north and the south," effectively filling the earth. This prophecy came to pass during the period known as the *Dispersion* when the Jews were scattered throughout the earth. It will be fulfilled more fully during the Millennial Kingdom when Christ reigns for a thousand years over the earth from Jerusalem.

15. BRING YOU BACK TO THIS LAND: God told Abraham that his descendants would be enslaved in a foreign land for four hundred years, after which time they would return to the promised land. (See Genesis 15:13–16.) This prophecy was fulfilled after the Israelites' exodus out of Egypt.

JACOB'S PICTURE OF GOD: *Jacob awakened after his dream and responded to the Lord's visit. But his response indicated that he did not understand the God of his fathers very well.*

16. THE LORD IS IN THIS PLACE: It seems that Jacob did not understand that God is everywhere at all times—He is omnipresent. He may have pictured God as moving about like a man, since that is the physical form He took on at least one occasion with Abraham. Jacob seemed to be saying here that God lives in Bethel and that if one moved away from Bethel, he would be moving away from God. There is no doubt that Jacob's understanding of God was limited at this point. He had much to learn concerning the God of his fathers.

18. SET IT UP AS A PILLAR: Marking a particular site as of special religious significance by means of a stone pillar was a known practice in Jacob's day. A libation offering (anointing the stone with oil), a change of place-name, and a vow of allegiance to the Lord in exchange for promised protection and blessing completed Jacob's ceremonial consecration of Bethel.

19. BETHEL: Meaning "house of God."

MAKING DEALS WITH GOD: *Though Jacob set up a pillar to commemorate God's visitation and even renamed the place, he was overcome with his own distrust and tried to bargain with God.*

---

20. IF GOD WILL BE WITH ME: God had just promised in the clearest terms that He would be with Jacob—yet Jacob was struggling to have faith in that promise. Abraham had a similar encounter with God; however, Abraham "believed in the LORD, and He accounted it to him for righteousness" (Genesis 15:6). It would appear that Isaac had not passed on to his son the truths of God's character that he himself experienced. Jacob was also hindered by his own bad character. He had been deceitful and treacherous to others, including his own twin brother, and he therefore expected others to treat him in the same way. Men who are not trustworthy have a very difficult time trusting others—including God, the only One who is absolutely trustworthy.

21. THEN THE LORD SHALL BE MY GOD: This is a response to God's miraculous appearance that we have not seen before. The Lord had just given Jacob a dramatic vision of Himself and had reiterated a promise He had given to Jacob's father and grandfather. If Jacob knew the facts of God's interactions with Abraham and Isaac and of the dramatic miracles that God had worked in the lives of his forebears—such as Isaac's miraculous birth and subsequent sacrifice—then we would expect him to bow in worship as Abraham had done. Instead, Jacob was trying to make a deal with God, effectively saying, "If You will keep Your promise, *then* I will make You my God—but not otherwise."

✍ READING GENESIS 32:7–13; 21–32 ✍

THE PAST CATCHES UP: *Years passed and Jacob and Laban eventually decided to part ways. Jacob journeyed with his wives and children to move back to Bethel, but along the way, he unexpectedly met his angry brother, Esau.*

7. JACOB WAS GREATLY AFRAID: Much time had passed in Jacob's life since his dream of God's ladder from heaven. He had cheated his father-in-law and been severely cheated in return, and over the years he had begun to learn some lessons in godliness. Now Jacob learned that his brother, Esau, was coming to meet him with four hundred men, and he was stricken with fear that Esau intended to kill him for his birthright treachery.

9. O God of my father Abraham: Up until now, Jacob had generally taken matters into his own hands, using whatever means he chose to accomplish his goals. But here we see a change of heart beginning: he was learning to call upon the name of God when he was in distress. It is also significant that he now addressed God as "God of my father Abraham and God of my father Isaac." It suggests that he had gained a deeper knowledge of the One whom he served, and it was also his first recorded prayer since his dream in Bethel.

10. I am not worthy: Jacob was learning humility. His lifelong habit of cunning and conniving had grown out of pride, a pride that led him to believe he could take charge of his own life without God's help. His previous encounter with God also demonstrated that pride, as he responded to God's grace by trying to make a deal. The wheeler-dealer is not apparent any longer.

11. Deliver me, I pray: Here we have a great breakthrough in Jacob's life. In the past he would have met such a crisis with cunning and craftiness; now he called upon his God to intervene on his behalf.

the hand of Esau: Jacob had good reason to be afraid, for he remembered the wicked way he treated his twin brother many years ago—and his brother's vow to kill him. (See Study 5 and Genesis 25 for more information.)

the mother with the children: Jacob expected that Esau would slaughter his entire household—men, women, and children. But it turns out he was not a good judge of character, as Esau had no such intentions. "But Esau ran to meet him, and embraced him, and fell on his neck and kissed him, and they wept" (Genesis 33:4). Men who spend their lives in deceit and treachery will generally expect others to behave the same way, thus causing them to be distrustful and suspicious of everyone. Jacob would never overcome this side effect to his own craftiness.

12. For You said: God likes to be reminded of His own words, and Jacob here reminds Him of His promise at Bethel. Again, this is the first time Jacob reminded God of these things or showed any real interest in submitting himself to God's plan.

Jacob Hides Behind the Women: *He next divided his household and flocks into two groups and sent them out ahead of him. Then he sent out his wives and children. He himself cowered behind.*

21. the present went on over before him: Jacob had put together a huge gift for Esau in hopes that the bribe would turn away his wrath. Jacob, of course, did not know that Esau was coming in friendship and forgiveness rather than vengeance. He could not expect Esau's reaction, for Jacob would never have done such a thing himself.

Indeed, he had sent on his family—his wives and children—to bear the brunt of Esau's wrath, while he shrank to the background. He had spent a lifetime developing this cowardly character, and its traits and habits would not disappear easily.

24. Jacob was left alone: This is the natural result of a life of treachery and selfishness; such a man will one day realize that he is completely alone. Fortunately for Jacob, however, he was not truly alone—the Lord had not deserted him, just as He promised. And there was also a certain pathos in this picture, as Jacob prayed in lonely exile the night before his ordeal.

Wrestling with God: *Suddenly we are confronted with a strange meeting, as God comes to Jacob—and Jacob wrestles Him to the ground. This provides an interesting contrast to Abraham.*

a Man wrestled with him: This Man was none other than God Himself. This appearance to Jacob was in stark contrast with God's appearance to Abraham in Mamre when Abraham interceded for the people of Sodom. (See Study 6 and Genesis 18.) Jacob did not stand before the Lord nor draw near to His face; he grappled and wrestled on the ground. He did not intercede for others; on the contrary, he sent others—women and children—out in front to intercede for him! Jacob was growing in godliness, but he was still a very self-centered man.

until the breaking of day: Again, this is a dramatic antithesis to Abraham's encounter with God. Abraham "wrestled" in a figurative sense with God, trying to understand the mind of his Creator. Jacob, however, spent the entire night trying to force *his* will onto God. This is how he lived his life, forcing his will upon others, and it had severely damaged his relationship with God and all those close to him.

Jacob Becomes Israel: *Jacob revealed the depth of his heart as he begged for God's blessing. God granted that boon and gave him a new name in the process.*

26. unless You bless me: But God had already blessed Jacob. The sad irony is that God appeared to Jacob this time in order to bless him still further. Nevertheless, we also see in this request where Jacob's heart lay: he longed for God's blessing and yearned to be a friend of God, as his grandfather Abraham had been. This is also what God saw in Jacob, looking beneath the conniving surface to the godly yearning in his heart.

28. you ... have prevailed: There is a positive example to be found in Jacob's wrestling, although it grew out of a character weakness in his case. Christians are exhorted to be fervent and persistent in prayer (see James 5:16; Luke 18), imitating Jacob's example of perseverance and tenacity.

30. Peniel: Meaning "face of God."

⤳ First Impressions ⤶

1. What does Jacob's dream mean? What is the ladder? Who or what are the angels going up and down the ladder?

2. What sort of neighbor might Jacob be if he lived near you? What would he be like as a co-worker or employee?

3. What would you have done if you had been in Jacob's place, anticipating that Esau was on his way to kill you?

4. Why did Jacob try to bargain with God after his dream? What does this show about his character? About his understanding of God?

⤳ Some Key Principles ⤶

When we insist upon taking matters into our own hands, we cheat ourselves of God's full blessing.

Jacob was a man of God, and he was the man who became known as Israel. He was blessed of God, yet he robbed himself of many more blessings that could have been his.

He lived a life marked by deceit and trickery, and that caused him to expect others to be deceitful and treacherous with him. As a result, he found it difficult to trust God. He doubted God's promises, and he attempted to secure a blessing by force that God wanted to give him freely. He stands in marked contrast to his grandfather Abraham, who took God at His word and found Him faithful.

We tend to expect others to treat us the way we treat others. If we tend to manipulate others into doing what we want, we will wind up unable to trust others—and God. God will still be faithful, but we will cheat ourselves of the blessings of intimacy and trust.

God still uses us despite our failures and weaknesses.

This is the "good news" part of the previous principle, and we can see it illustrated in Jacob's life. Jacob was a man with many obvious weaknesses and shortcomings, and from a human perspective, he was not the sort of man that most people would trust. But God was still able to use him in mighty ways, and he is listed among the heroes of the faith.

"The LORD does not see as man sees; for man looks at the outward appearance, but the LORD looks at the heart" (1 Samuel 16:7). The Lord looked on the heart of Jacob and found a man who ultimately longed for His blessing and intimacy.

When we have a relationship with our Creator, He instills within us character traits that are pleasing to Him. Through His Spirit He develops those things in us, making us more like Christ as we grow. This process may not always be pleasant, but in the end we will reflect the image of His Son.

Parents must teach their children about God's character.

Jacob's early responses to God seem to suggest that he had little knowledge of God's character. His verbal response was closer to a business deal than to worship and praise.

This was radically different from the responses of his grandfather Abraham, who had a clear understanding of the persona and character of the Lord. Somewhere along the line, it would appear that Jacob had not been taught very clearly about God. Perhaps Isaac forgot to teach him about all the things that he had seen God do in his own life and in Abraham's life. As a result, it took Jacob a lifetime to discover the fullness of God's grace and mercy, and he wasted a lot of time wrestling against both God and man.

Each person must come to repentance and salvation for himself—the fact that a parent is a Christian does not guarantee the salvation of his children. Yet parents who teach their children about God's love and salvation lay a critical spiritual foundation for their children. In faithfully teaching their kids about the gospel, they pass on a genuine blessing and "birthright" to their children.

﹌ DIGGING DEEPER ﹌

5. Why did Jacob wrestle with God? Why did God consent to wrestle with Jacob?

6. What might have happened if Jacob had not wrestled with God? What sort of meeting might they have had? Why did Jacob's stubborn, manipulative character make a wrestling match necessary?

7. Why do you think God gave Jacob a limp during the wrestling match? In what ways did Jacob's limp serve as a constant reminder of his weakness and of his need to depend on God?

8. Given Jacob's untrustworthy character, why did God bless him? In what ways did Jacob experience the fruit of his sinfulness?

﹌ TAKING IT PERSONALLY ﹌

9. Is there an area in your life where you are wrestling against God? How can you let go and trust Him more fully?

10. Are there ways that "wrestling" with God is a good thing? What does this teach us about prayer?

SECTION 3:

THEMES

In This Section:

~ 10 ~
COVENANT AND OBEDIENCE

ᔑ THEMATIC BACKGROUND ᔐ

In Study 2, we witnessed the Lord making a covenant with Abram concerning his descendants and their future in the land of Canaan. That covenant was unconditional; God alone promised it to Abram and sealed it with a ritual involving animal sacrifice. Abram didn't need to do anything in the process except be a witness.

Later, however, God came to Abram again and reiterated that covenant. This time God emphasized Abraham's need to keep the covenant and revealed what the sign of the covenant would be—namely, circumcision. The rite of circumcision (which involved the removal of the male foreskin) set the Jewish people apart as those specially chosen by God. It also symbolized the need to cut away sin and be cleansed. God commanded Abraham and his descendants to keep the covenant that He had made with them.

Sadly, there were many times throughout Israel's history that the nation was unfaithful to this covenant and the other covenants that God had made with them. Nonetheless, God's faithfulness to the Abrahamic Covenant never wavered.

This passage again underscores the intimate fellowship that Abraham enjoyed with God. We saw some of this in Study 6, where Abraham stood and spoke to God face-to-face, as a friend to a friend. He received something else in this passage: a new name. God changed his name from Abram to Abraham. His wife also received a new name, going from Sarai to Sarah. These new names symbolized the fact that God had a special purpose for Abram and Sarai—as the parents of His chosen nation.

In this study, we will look at the historical event of God's covenant with Abraham; then we will move into the New Testament to find out what it all means to us today.

ᔑ READING GENESIS 17:1–27 ᔐ

GOD SPEAKS TO ABRAM: *We will begin at the time just before Isaac was born when Abram was ninety-nine and Sarai eighty-nine. God appears to Abram once again, probably in a dream or vision.*

1. Abram was ninety-nine years old: Once again, we are back at the point just prior to the birth of Isaac. This conversation between God and Abram (who would become Abraham) took place just before God's visit on His way to Sodom when Abraham interceded for Lot and the Sodomites. The location of this event was probably Mamre.

the Lord appeared to Abram: We are not told in this case just *how* God appeared to Abram, but it was most likely in the form of a dream or a vision. We do know that He appeared previously in dreams and visions (e.g., Genesis 15:1, 12). It is likely that God had *not* appeared in physical form to Abraham up to this time, as He would do when He came in physical form to judge Sodom in Genesis 18.

walk before Me: The Hebrew word translated "before Me" means "face." God was saying, "Walk in My face—keep My face before you at all times, and remember that My face is always looking toward you."

be blameless: This word means "complete, whole, having integrity." God did not expect Abraham to live a sin-free life from that point on but that his life would be characterized by patterns of righteousness. Similarly, God does not expect that Christians will never again fall into sin after salvation. He does, however, command us to order our entire lives around His Word. Moreover, we have been covered in the righteousness of Christ and our sins have been cleansed because of His death on our behalf.

New Names: *God signifies His special purposes for Abram—as the father of His chosen people—by giving him and Sarai new names.*

2. I will make My covenant between Me and you: This is a reiteration of the covenant that God made earlier with Abraham. In Genesis 15, God simply performed a ritual for Abraham that sealed His unwavering commitment to fulfill the promises to Abraham and Abraham's descendants. But this time God introduced the sign of that covenant—circumcision.

4. My covenant is with you: God had already established His covenant with Abraham in chapter 15, in which He promised that Abraham's descendants would be countless and that they would inherit the land of Canaan. Now he reaffirmed that promise again after many years had passed.

5. Abram . . . Abraham: Abram means "high father," while Abraham means "father of many nations." It is very significant that God gave Abraham a new name, because it underscored the fact that God had a special purpose for Abraham as the father of His chosen people. In ancient times, a ruler, for instance, might assign a subject a new name to indicate that the subject was now his property. This was likewise true of Abraham, who was God's choice servant—a man whom God would use to bring great blessing to the world.

4–8: The Lord here reiterated the elements of the covenant He had been promising to Abraham for nearly twenty-five years: many descendants, the land of Canaan, and becoming a blessing to the nations.

REAFFIRMING THE COVENANT: *The Lord already made this covenant with Abram, but in this passage some very important details are added—details that will instruct Abraham and his descendants as to how they are to respond to God's gracious promises.*

7. I WILL ESTABLISH MY COVENANT: The unique relationship between God and Abraham was one that God initiated. He was the one who chose Abraham, not the other way around.

AN EVERLASTING COVENANT: God's special relationship with Abraham's descendants will last as long as the earth itself, and even into eternity. This promise will be realized in its fullness during the future Millennial Kingdom, when Jesus Christ reigns on the earth for a thousand years. At that time, all of Israel will be saved. (See Romans 11:26.)

8. ALL THE LAND OF CANAAN: God's reaffirmation of His covenant promises to Abraham did not occur without mention of the land being deeded by divine right to him and his descendants as an everlasting possession.

9. YOU SHALL KEEP MY COVENANT: Despite repeated disobedience by the patriarchs and the nation, God's faithfulness to His covenant commitment never wavered. Though the nation would be characterized by times of disobedience, God was true to His Word. There was always an obedient remnant of faithful Israelites, who walked in the example of their father Abraham.

10. THIS IS MY COVENANT WHICH YOU SHALL KEEP: Now the Lord defined the new covenant.

CIRCUMCISION: *In reiterating His covenant with Abraham, God institutes the sign of that covenant: circumcision.*

CIRCUMCISED: Circumcision is the removal of the male foreskin. See the notes on Colossians below for more discussion on this important rite.

11. IT SHALL BE A SIGN OF THE COVENANT: There was nothing magical about this operation; being circumcised did not bring about some mystical transformation in the male or purchase a relationship with God. It was done solely as an outward sign of the covenant, just as a wedding ring is the outward sign of a marriage covenant.

12. EIGHT DAYS OLD: From a medical perspective, this is the ideal time to perform this operation, since it heals quickly and produces the least pain possible. But it also suggests that it is good for a person to commit himself to the Lord at an early age. "It is good for a man to bear the yoke in his youth" (Lamentations 3:27).

EVERY MALE CHILD IN YOUR GENERATIONS: Here we see again the importance of parental teaching concerning the ways of the Lord. Circumcision represents a decision that each man must make for himself—whether or not to serve the Lord faithfully—yet it is also a decision that is made by the parents for the child. Parents bear a very significant share of the responsibility for the spiritual decisions their children will make. (See Study 9.)

13. MUST BE CIRCUMCISED: The Lord now underscored this principle even further, making it clear that His people are accountable to ensure that their entire household is brought under the teaching of God's Word. Fathers are held to a high degree of accountability concerning the spiritual welfare of their entire families. Parents bear a very significant share of the responsibility for helping their children make wise spiritual decisions.

14. THAT PERSON SHALL BE CUT OFF: A person's relationship with God is a very serious business. The Lord was making it clear that any one of the Israelites who was not willing to obey Him in this important way evidenced the fact that he was not a true follower of God. Thus he should be distanced from those who willingly submitted to God's commands. To be cut off meant to be disinherited and disowned, removed from the presence of God and His people.

HE HAS BROKEN MY COVENANT: This did not mean that Abraham's descendants would not inherit the land; it meant that any of Abraham's descendants who were uncircumcised would not inherit a relationship with God.

15. SARAI . . . SARAH: Sarai can mean "my princess," whereas Sarah means "princess." This is a subtle distinction, perhaps indicating that as the mother of many nations, she would become a princess to more than just her husband. The bigger issue, however, is that the Lord was changing her name as well as her husband's, indicating that she, too, was chosen by God for a special purpose.

GOD'S WAY OR NO WAY: *The Lord once again made it apparent that He had one chosen seed, and only one, through whom the promise would be fulfilled.*

18. OH, THAT ISHMAEL MIGHT LIVE BEFORE YOU!: Abraham was struggling to comprehend how God was going to give him a son through Sarah at their advanced ages. He was struggling with doubt, which we have already considered in Study 7. His doubting mind resorted to an easy solution: Ishmael, who had already been born. But God is not hindered by simple impossibilities, and He had a good reason for rejecting Ishmael or any other person except the one of His choosing.

19. I will establish My covenant with him: Once again we are confronted with the fact that God was sovereignly at work in determining through whom He would bring about His chosen seed. Abraham had other sons, just as Isaac would have two sons. But the covenant of God would not extend to "other sons"—only to the one chosen from each generation. This foreshadowed the fact that there is ultimately only one way to find peace with God, and that is through His only begotten Son—the final Chosen Seed of Israel's race.

⤳ Reading Colossians 2:9–14 ⤳

The Deity of Christ: *Paul also addressed the issue of circumcision and how it applies to Christians, but he opened his discussion with a major point: Jesus is God.*

9. all the fullness of the Godhead bodily: Jesus is God, part of the Trinity of the Godhead. Many cults claim that Jesus was the *Son* of God without actually being part of the Godhead. This, however, denies a fundamental doctrine of the Christian church. If Jesus is not God, then He cannot forgive sin, because all sin is against God. (See Psalm 51:4.) If Jesus is not God, then all that Paul was saying in this chapter is null and void.

10. you are complete in Him: This ties back to God's covenant with Abraham, where the Lord commanded Abraham, "I am Almighty God; walk before Me and be blameless" (Genesis 17:1). (The word *blameless* means to be complete; see notes on 17:1 above.) Through the sacrificial death of Jesus, we are now blameless and complete in the eyes of the Father—our entire debt has been paid, and we are washed as clean as if we had never sinned.

Spiritual Circumcision: *Abraham's circumcision was merely a physical picture of a deeper spiritual truth. Paul now tells us what it symbolized.*

11. the circumcision made without hands: The circumcision of the Old Testament law was merely a physical picture of an eternal, spiritual truth. Circumcision symbolized man's need for cleansing of the heart and was the outward sign of that cleansing of sin that comes by faith in God. In Christ, this eternal truth is fulfilled—made complete—in each person who accepts Him as Savior. At salvation, believers undergo a spiritual "circumcision" by "putting off the body of the sins of the flesh." This is the new birth, the new creation in conversion.

PUTTING OFF THE BODY OF THE SINS OF THE FLESH: Circumcision involved cutting off the male foreskin, which was representative of the fact that the sinful nature (which is transmitted through the seed of the man) must be cut off. By cutting off this piece of flesh, Old Testament Jews were symbolizing the fact that God required His people to "cut off" the "flesh"—that is, to completely remove the sinful nature. Of course, a person cannot actually physically cut off his human nature, since we are born into the flesh of Adam. Thus, physical circumcision could not eternally save anyone; it was merely a picture of spiritual truths.

THE CIRCUMCISION OF CHRIST: Circumcision could not save anyone, because it did not alter the fact that a person is born into Adam's sinful line and bears his sinful nature. No man can change that—but God can! Only God can offer a person a *new* birth into the *new* Adam (being Christ), a new life that is devoid of Adam's sinful nature. This is the "circumcision of Christ," which provides a new birth for anyone who accepts Him as Lord and Savior.

12. RAISED WITH HIM THROUGH FAITH: Once the Adamic nature has been put to death, we are raised into a new birth, which for Christians is symbolized in baptism when we come out of the water as Christ burst out of the tomb.

13. HAVING FORGIVEN YOU ALL TRESPASSES: Again, only God can forgive sin, so Jesus has to be God if the New Testament is to be proved true. This teaching is the very reason the Jews wanted to crucify Christ. "And the scribes and the Pharisees began to reason, saying, 'Who is this who speaks blasphemies? Who can forgive sins but God alone?'" (Luke 5:21). "Therefore the Jews sought all the more to kill Him, because He not only broke the Sabbath, but also said that God was His Father, making Himself equal with God" (John 5:18).

ᨕ FIRST IMPRESSIONS ᨕ

1. *Why did God reiterate His covenant with Abram? What additional information did God provide Abram on this occasion?*

2. Why did God command Abraham to have all the males in his household circumcised? Why not just Abraham alone?

3. Why did God rename Abram and Sarai? What does this symbolize?

4. What did physical circumcision symbolize for the Old Testament Jew? What spiritual reality did circumcision represent?

✦ Some Key Principles ✦

The flesh cannot inherit the kingdom of God.

When the Bible speaks about the flesh, it is referring to our sinful nature. We have inherited our human flesh from Adam, the father of the human race. Unfortunately, we inherited more than just Adam's physical flesh—we also inherited his decision to commit sin. Genesis makes it clear that "like brings forth like," meaning that one type of creature can only reproduce its own kind. That means that Adam and his descendants can only give birth to sinners because they are sinners themselves.

God cannot tolerate the presence of sin in any degree whatsoever. This is a terrible situation for Adam's descendants to be in, because we are born in sin and cannot escape our human heritage—and therefore we are eternally cut off from the presence of God.

There is only one hope for mankind: we must find some way of removing our sinful nature—our flesh—if we are to enter God's presence. This is precisely what the Lord was symbolizing when He commanded Abraham to be circumcised. The fulfillment of this symbol came several thousand years later through God's Son, Jesus Christ.

Christians are born again into the Second Adam.

This leads us into the next principle, which is that Jesus made possible what for man was impossible, that is a change in our nature—something that is utterly impossible under the laws of creation. "A leopard cannot change its spots," as the old saying goes, and neither can a man change the fact that he is born in the image of Adam.

God makes this miracle possible by offering us the opportunity to be born *again* into a new image, born a second time to the Second Adam, God's Son Jesus Christ. (See 1 Corinthians 15:45.) In order to be born again, however, our old self must first die. These truths are symbolized in baptism. To symbolize dying to our flesh, we go down into the water (as Christ went into the tomb in death) as the old man, the old Adam. To symbolize our rebirth through the power of the Spirit, we come up out of the water (as Christ burst out of the tomb) into the person of the new man, the family of the Last Adam, being reborn through the power of the Spirit.

When we accept Christ as Savior, we put to death our sinful nature and are born again into a new nature, into the image of Christ. And just as we could not remove our original natures by our own efforts, so also we can never lose our new nature—we are reborn forever into the image of God's Son, Jesus Christ.

Jesus is God.

This truth is absolute bedrock to the Christian faith. Only God can forgive sins, so the One who offers forgiveness of sins must be God if that offer is to be real. Only God can "change the leopard's spots," removing our Adamic nature and giving us a new God-nature.

Groups who teach that Jesus is not God—such as the Mormons and Jehovah's Witnesses—are preaching a false gospel. The New Testament is very clear on the deity of Christ, as Paul demonstrated in our passages in this study. (See Colossians 2:9.) Jesus Himself forgave the sins of His followers (e.g., Luke 5:21), and He accepted the worship of men who proclaimed Him God (e.g., John 20:28).

It is vital that Christians understand and cling to this important fact, for it is at the very basis of our faith. When we proclaim Jesus as Lord, we are proclaiming Him as Creator God.

↶ Digging Deeper ↶

5.   What does it mean to be "born again"? What is involved in becoming born again?

6.   How do we know that Jesus is God? Give scriptural support.

7.   Why did God not command Sarah to do something in His reiteration of the covenant? What does this teach about spiritual headship?

8.   Considering that God's promise involved giving birth to a son, why is it significant that Abraham had to be circumcised before that promise was fulfilled?

9. Have you been born again? If not, why? What have you got to lose? What have you got to gain?

10. If you are a Christian, have you been baptized? If not, why? What is holding you back from obeying this command of Scripture and publicly symbolizing your union with Christ?

11

TRUSTING EVERYTHING TO GOD

GENESIS 48; HEBREWS 11

✦ THEMATIC BACKGROUND ✦

Faith has been one of the major themes in all the passages we have studied, and we have seen that it is faith that produces righteousness. But what exactly *is* faith? And how does one live *by* faith? These phrases are easy to use, but precisely how are they lived out in real life?

We have already examined the lives of many people who did this very thing, including Abraham, Sarah, and Jacob. These men and women were not perfect, and their lives certainly included times when they failed to live by faith—but each of them ended his or her days with a deep faith in God.

Faith is a verb, an action word—something that is done or acted out, not felt or merely believed. Faith is the carrying into practice of one's deepest beliefs. If we believe in the character of God, then we will carry that belief into practice, building our lives upon the assurance of God's faithfulness. This is the essence of faith.

We will begin our study with Jacob, picking up near the end of his life. We will then move into the New Testament and examine the great "faith chapter" of the Bible, Hebrews 11. The writer of Hebrews will help us understand what it means to live by faith and what motivated the patriarchs to do so.

Perhaps Abraham gave us the most striking picture of what it means to live by faith when he went to sacrifice Isaac on the altar. He did this because he completely trusted that God would keep His promises—and those promises required that Isaac be alive. He recognized that God could even go so far as to raise Isaac back from the dead if needed.

Abraham demonstrated faith, because he trusted everything to God.

✦ READING GENESIS 48:8–10 ✦

JACOB FINISHES IN FAITH: *We'll begin this study by returning to Jacob, visiting him at the very end of his life. We will discover that the one who wrestled against God actually finished in faith.*

8. ISRAEL SAW JOSEPH'S SONS: Israel was Jacob's new name (see Genesis 32:28), and this passage takes place near the end of his life after his son Joseph has become second-in-command of Egypt.

9. I WILL BLESS THEM: We now see that Jacob did indeed grow into a godly man of faith, more like his grandfather Abraham than he was in his earlier life that we saw in Study 9. He was now passing on the godly blessing, just as his father Isaac had done for him.

10. HE COULD NOT SEE: He was evidently leaning on his staff, a bent and aged man. His physical eyes could not see any longer, but his spiritual eyes had been opened by the Lord. The author of Hebrews further developed this theme.

⤳ READING HEBREWS 11:1–2 ⤳

WHAT IS FAITH?: *Hebrews 11 is known as the "faith chapter," because it focuses on men and women of Scripture whose lives exemplified what it means to live by faith.*

1. FAITH: This concept of faith has been a unifying thread throughout our studies. In this chapter, the author of Hebrews develops and expounds on what exactly faith means. The dictionary defines faith as "confidence, reliance, belief, especially without evidence or proof; belief based on testimony or authority."[1] This passage, however, will add much more insight to that definition.

THE SUBSTANCE OF THINGS HOPED FOR: The word *hope* in Scripture means much more than wishing fervently for something—which is how we generally use the word in everyday speech. The New Testament uses the word *hope* to mean a confident anticipation of something that will assuredly occur in the future, as certain as tomorrow's sunrise. "But if we hope for what we do not see, we eagerly wait for it with perseverance" (Romans 8:25). Our *faith* is the "substance" of those things that we confidently anticipate, which this passage will define further.

THE EVIDENCE OF THINGS NOT SEEN: This means that our faith is actually a proof to the world around us of the truth of those things which are "not seen." Abraham was a witness to the world around him that God could bring the dead back to life when he had faith in God, demonstrated by sacrificing his son Isaac. Thus, Abraham's faith gave evidence to the world of things not seen. True faith is not based upon the evidence of our senses, but on the character of God. We have faith because we trust Him.

---

1. Leslie Brown, ed., *The New Shorter Oxford English Dictionary*, (Oxford: Clarendon Press, 1993).

108

2. THE ELDERS OBTAINED A GOOD TESTIMONY: The "elders" are the men and women of faith whose lives are examined in Hebrews 11. They are the saints whose lives provide us today with "a good testimony," an example that we can imitate of living a life of faith.

⌒ READING HEBREWS 11:6–21 ⌒

HOW TO PLEASE GOD: *The first thing we must understand is that God wants His people to live by faith. We cannot hope to please Him otherwise.*

6. WITHOUT FAITH IT IS IMPOSSIBLE TO PLEASE HIM: It is impossible to please God unless we come into His presence; a person who remains apart from God will never please Him. But we cannot enter His presence unless we first exercise faith in Him.

HE WHO COMES TO GOD MUST BELIEVE THAT HE IS: This seems fairly self-evident. If a person wishes to enter the presence of God, he must first believe that God exists. Yet it is an ironic absurdity that people will frequently talk about eternal values and everlasting happiness, while simultaneously denying that God exists. "The fool has said in his heart, 'There is no God'" (Psalm 14:1).

HE IS A REWARDER OF THOSE WHO DILIGENTLY SEEK HIM: This is the second requirement for those who wish to enter God's presence. Once again, it is an act of faith based on the character of God. We seek His presence because we believe that He exists and that our sincere pursuit of Him will not be disappointed.

ABRAHAM THE PILGRIM: *Abraham is listed as a man of faith because he followed God without any knowledge of where God was leading him.*

8. BY FAITH ABRAHAM OBEYED: Abraham obeyed God because God made him a promise. He accepted God's word on that promise and acted in faith that He would fulfill it.

NOT KNOWING WHERE HE WAS GOING: God only told Abraham to head south from Haran, moving "to a land that I will show you" (Genesis 12:1). In doing so, Abraham demonstrated the definition of faith from verse 1 by believing that God would provide him a home and an inheritance, without seeing it first. He believed when there was a complete absence of physical proof and based his trust solely on God's character.

9. HE DWELT IN THE LAND OF PROMISE AS IN A FOREIGN COUNTRY: It was hard enough to leave his home and family without knowing where he was going, but he then was called upon to live the remainder of his life without actually receiving that promised land! Instead, he traveled to and fro in the land as though he were a rootless stranger, when in fact he was destined to be the land's owner.

DWELLING IN TENTS: It is quite likely that Abraham and his household had lived in permanent homes before traveling to Canaan. Here is yet another test of his faith, as he must have looked back sometimes to what he had left behind, wondering why he had given up so much to attain what appeared to be so little.

10. HE WAITED FOR THE CITY WHICH HAS FOUNDATIONS: And here is the secret to Abraham's great faith: he was anticipating—he was *hoping for*—a different city, something that was in the future, a city that could not be seen or perceived with earthly senses. This city "has foundations" that are not on earth but in eternity, a "heavenly Jerusalem" (see Revelation 21:2, 14) whose architect and builder is God Himself. This is what is meant by *hope*, for Abraham looked forward to this city with a confident anticipation that it shall come to pass.

SARAH FOUND STRENGTH: *Sarah also demonstrated a life of faith simply because she believed what God told her, judging that He was faithful.*

11. RECEIVED STRENGTH: Sarah received the strength to conceive when her body was far beyond the point of conception. Yet God also strengthened her faith itself, enabling her to trust Him even more than she had. This is another of God's great mercies toward His people—He requires faith to please Him, yet He helps us to have that faith in the first place. "Immediately the father of the child cried out and said with tears, 'Lord, I believe; help my unbelief!'" (Mark 9:24).

BECAUSE SHE JUDGED HIM FAITHFUL WHO HAD PROMISED: Here again we discover the core of faith. Sarah had faith, not in the evidence of her senses (which told her that conception was impossible) but in the character of God. She believed the promise because she believed the One who *made* the promise.

12. HIM AS GOOD AS DEAD: Once again, the evidence of the senses told Abraham that God's promise was absolutely impossible: a hundred-year-old man could not expect to have a child with a ninety-year-old woman! But faith is acting on one's understanding of the character of God, not on the evidence that one can see in the world or in circumstances.

THE STARS OF THE SKY IN MULTITUDE—INNUMERABLE AS THE SAND WHICH IS BY THE SEASHORE: This was God's original promise to Abraham, yet he never saw it fulfilled in his own lifetime. But the promise of countless descendants has been fulfilled quite literally, not merely in the people of Israel but also in the people of Christ—for Christians are also counted as spiritual descendants of Abraham.

FINISHING WELL: *Each of the patriarchs lived a life of faith—and died without seeing the full completion of God's promises.*

13. DIED IN FAITH: The man or woman of God will live by faith consistently and for the long term. We are called to "finish the race" and to finish it well. "Do you not know that those who run in a race all run, but one receives the prize? Run in such a way that you may obtain it" (1 Corinthians 9:24).

NOT HAVING RECEIVED THE PROMISES: As we have seen throughout these studies, the men and women of faith in Genesis lived out their lives without ever seeing the complete fulfillment of God's promises. Some parts of His promises did come to pass, such as the birth of Isaac, but none of the people that we've studied ever inherited the promised land. Yet they continued in faith despite not seeing the completion of God's plan, because they trusted in His faithfulness to keep His promises.

THEY WERE STRANGERS AND PILGRIMS ON THE EARTH: Here we find the secret to this great faith: these men and women of God kept their eyes focused on the eternal things of God rather than on the temporal things of this earth. Christians must remember that we are merely pilgrims in this world, only here temporarily. This world is not our home; like Abraham, we look forward to an eternal home that is not built with human hands.

OUR FAITH IS A WITNESS: *When we live by faith, the world around us sees that faith and is convicted by our testimony that God is faithful.*

14. DECLARE PLAINLY: We live by faith because we have our eyes fixed on Jesus, "the author and finisher of our faith" (Hebrews 12:2), and therefore our attention is fixed in an upward, eternal direction. But that faith has results in an outward, temporal direction as well, because the people around us can see our faith and recognize where our hope lies. In this way, the faith of God's people declares plainly to the world around us that God is real and that He is a rewarder of those who diligently seek Him.

15. IF THEY HAD CALLED TO MIND THAT COUNTRY FROM WHICH THEY HAD COME OUT: That is, if Abraham had shifted his focus to his father's house in Haran or Ur, the places that he left when God called him, then he might have become tempted by the temporal values of the world around him. This faith requires that we place our priorities on eternal things—and that we continually work to keep them there. It is a discipline that must be renewed daily, for the cares and necessities of the world will continually try to draw our focus away from the things of God. Notice that the secret has to do with what we "call to mind"—it is an attitude of our thinking that controls where our priorities will lie. "Do not be conformed to this world, but be transformed by the renewing of your mind, that you may prove what is that good and acceptable and perfect will of God" (Romans 12:2).

THEY WOULD HAVE HAD OPPORTUNITY TO RETURN: This is where the struggle lies in leading a life of faith, for we will always face the temptation to turn our eyes away from Christ and look at the world around us. The renewing of our minds is a daily exercise, one that we must renew frequently through the study of God's Word and Christian fellowship. "Let us hold fast the confession of our hope without wavering, for He who promised is faithful. And let us consider one another in order to stir up love and good works, not forsaking the assembling of ourselves together, as is the manner of some, but exhorting one another, and so much the more as you see the Day approaching" (Hebrews 10:23–25).

GOD IS HONORED THROUGH HIS PEOPLE: *We must have faith to enter God's presence, but when we do have faith, we do more than just please Him—we bring honor and glory to Him.*

16. GOD IS NOT ASHAMED TO BE CALLED THEIR GOD: It is impossible to please God without faith, but those who place their faith in God do more than please Him— they bring Him honor. He is pleased to be known as their God and eager to proclaim that they are His children.

19. GOD WAS ABLE TO RAISE HIM UP: This is the reason Abraham was able to travel to Moriah to sacrifice his beloved son without argument. The whole time he was anticipating with confidence that God would keep His promises concerning his descendants—even to the point of raising Isaac from the dead. Abraham was able to act in faith because he had a fervent hope, built upon the faithful character of God.

ᔕ FIRST IMPRESSIONS ᔕ

1. *Make a list of acts of faith for each of the following people. What can we learn from each?*
Abraham:

Sarah:

Isaac:

Jacob:

2.   *Define faith in your own words.*

3.   *In practical terms, what does it mean to "trust everything to God"? What specifically is included in "everything"?*

4.   *How were the patriarchs "strangers and pilgrims" on earth? Why were they called to this?*

﹌ Some Key Principles ﹌

We must run the race in faith—and we must finish in faith.

Jesus told a parable about a man who sowed seed in a field. (See Matthew 13.) Some of that seed grew up into a rich harvest because it finished its purpose, but other seeds did not produce any harvest because they did not finish what had been started. This is an important principle for God's people to keep in mind: we must live by faith, and we must *continue* to live by faith as long as the Lord chooses to keep us on earth.

Paul used the metaphor of a person who is running in a footrace. That runner might begin the race with great zeal, but somewhere along the route he begins to grow weary. He cannot hope to win the race unless he *finishes* well. We see this in the men and women whom we have examined in these studies. They may have stumbled along the way, but the general pattern of their lives was that of living by faith.

"But also for this very reason, giving all diligence, add to your faith virtue, to virtue knowledge, to knowledge self-control, to self-control perseverance, to perseverance godliness" (2 Peter 1:5–6). "But he who endures to the end shall be saved" (Matthew 24:13).

This world is not our home.

It is vital that Christians keep this truth in mind, for we are called to keep our eyes focused on eternity rather than on the world. But the world has a way of insinuating itself and its values into our thinking. Careers, academics, bills, obligations, even family will all demand our time and attention; this is a fact of life and cannot be entirely avoided while we live in the world. But we must also remember that we are *in* the world but not *of* the world—our home is in eternity.

This mind-set is one that must be renewed frequently, because the world around us will not give up the battle for our minds. We renew our minds by immersing ourselves in Scripture and by surrounding ourselves with other Christians who are like-minded. We reinforce the mind-set by prayerfully remembering, whenever we are tempted to worry or covet, that we are not going to be living on this planet forever.

We are citizens of a heavenly city, one that is not built by human hands and one that will last forever. Everything in this world—absolutely everything—will one day be destroyed by fire, and we must take care not to invest our lives into things that will be burned up.

Faith is determined by the character of God, not by the evidence of our senses.

Abraham, Sarah, Jacob, and many others believed in things that seemed absurdly impossible. They did more than believe; they *acted* upon those beliefs—and that acting out of their beliefs is what we call faith.

That faith, however, was not from a "wishful thinking" that maybe someday the impossible would occur. It was based upon an utter conviction that God is faithful and that His promises are certain. Indeed, these men and women of faith were faithful only because God was faithful first. Their faith was an imitation of God's character.

Our faith is not founded on the evidence of modern science or the substantiation of our senses or anything else in this temporal world. Our faith is built upon the character of God; we have absolute hope and faith that He will keep His promises because we know that He is faithful—"being confident of this very thing, that He who has begun a good work in you will complete it until the day of Jesus Christ" (Philippians 1:6).

5. What does it mean to "finish the race well"? How is this accomplished?

6. What things make it difficult to keep our eyes focused on eternity? Give real-life examples.

7. When have you seen God's faithfulness in your own life? How can these experiences help you trust Him in the future?

8. How does a Christian strike a balance between responsibility to the obligations of life and staying focused on eternity?

ᓚ Taking It Personally ᓗ

9. Is your life characterized more by faith in God or by looking out for your own interests? How can you deepen your trust in God?

10. If you could accomplish only one thing in your lifetime, what would it be? Does this goal reflect a heavenly focus or an earthly focus?

SECTION 4:

SUMMARY

NOTES AND PRAYER REQUESTS

12

REVIEWING KEY PRINCIPLES

⤙ LOOKING BACK ⤚

We have examined the lives of the great patriarchs of the faith: Abraham, Isaac, and Jacob (Israel) and have seen how each of them learned to walk by faith rather than by sight. Each of these people had strengths and weaknesses, and each was made of the same flesh that we are made of. They were all people just like us, struggling with the realities of life in a fallen world and learning to trust in their faithful Creator.

The major theme of these studies has been on the life of faith, looking at what is required to live by faith and what is gained by such a lifestyle. The central tenet of this lifestyle is to trust in the character of God, not in the evidences of our senses or the circumstances of the world around us. God is always faithful, and He will always keep His promises. Those promises include an eternal life in His kingdom, blessed with His presence for all eternity. This is available through His Son, Jesus Christ, who through the Cross provides the only way to peace with God.

Here are a few of the major themes we have found. There are many more that we don't have room to reiterate, so take some time to review the earlier studies—or better still, to meditate upon the passages in Scripture that we have covered. Ask the Holy Spirit to give you wisdom and insight into His Word.

⤙ SOME KEY PRINCIPLES ⤚

God calls His people to walk in faith.

Each of the characters we have looked at in these studies was called upon to believe the promises of God—promises that appeared to be utterly impossible. God then asked them to take some action based upon those promises, and this action is what we call "walking in faith."

This is what it means to walk in faith: to step into the unknown, even into threatening circumstances, with only God's Word to depend on. Abram arrived in Canaan to find himself surrounded with unfriendly people, and God then told him that he would inherit the entire land for his descendants. Later he was called upon to sacrifice his son, even though all God's promises for the future depended upon that son.

Walking in faith requires that we accept God's Word at face value, even when it seems impossible that His promises can come true. In this, the patriarchs provide us with great role models.

God works all things together for good to those who trust Him.

This principle is closely related to the previous one, in that we are called to trust and obey. But the good news is that God's long-term plans for the human race do not override His short-term plans for us as individuals.

God's promises to Abraham focused more on his descendants than they did on him personally. The land of Canaan was promised to his offspring, but he personally never received any place that he could call home. But at the same time, Abraham was given something far greater than any piece of real estate: he was granted a saving relationship with God Himself.

The Lord does use His people to further His purposes in the lives of others, but He also pours out blessings upon those people as He uses them. The greatest blessing of all is free to God's people today, just as it was for Abraham: an intimate communion with the Creator of all things.

The comforts of the world can become a deadly trap.

Lot did not leave Abram and head straight for a new house in Sodom; he arrived there by degrees. So it is with the comforts and entanglements of the world—they grow upon us a little at a time.

This is a difficult balance, because the Lord's people are called to be in the world but not of the world. We have no choice but to live in society and take part in the workaday economy, yet we must also be on guard to ensure that these entanglements do not become the focus of our lives.

"Do not love the world or the things in the world. If anyone loves the world, the love of the Father is not in him. For all that is in the world—the lust of the flesh, the lust of the eyes, and the pride of life—is not of the Father but is of the world. And the world is passing away, and the lust of it; but he who does the will of God abides forever" (1 John 2:15–17).

God sometimes calls us to costly obedience.

There is no question that Abraham was severely tested by God's command to sacrifice his beloved son. Yet God is not frivolous; this command was not just some random test. His purpose was to prove the strength of Abraham's faith—and a great deal more. He also wanted to present to the world a picture of His plan to sacrifice His own Son on the cross.

He will sometimes ask His children, even in modern times, to obey Him in ways that are very costly. Sometimes obedience to His Word requires great personal sacrifice. But we can be confident that obedience is more valuable than anything this world has to offer. Moreover, costly obedience leads to eternal riches, as we saw in our look at Hebrews 11.

God never gives us tests we cannot pass.

God "knows our frame; He remembers that we are dust" (Psalm 103:14). He sends tests into our lives in order to strengthen us, to build Christlike character in our lives—not to find fault with us or to seek an excuse to punish us. His tests are designed for us to pass, not to fail.

Of course, when we are in the middle of a trial, it can seem overwhelming and unbearable. At such times, we must remember that Christians have God's Holy Spirit within us, working right alongside of us to help us through the trials and tribulations of life. There are times when we are called upon to patiently endure, to accept a trial or hardship as from the hand of God without trying to manipulate the circumstances in order to contrive our own solutions.

"My brethren, count it all joy when you fall into various trials, knowing that the testing of your faith produces patience" (James 1:2–3). "No temptation has overtaken you except such as is common to man; but God is faithful, who will not allow you to be tempted beyond what you are able, but with the temptation will also make the way of escape, that you may be able to bear it" (1 Corinthians 10:13).

We are all called to be friends of God.

It is easy to become complacent about this concept, to take for granted what a priceless treasure we have in our relationship with God through Christ. When we pray, we are entering freely into the very presence of the Creator of the universe! This is a privilege that came at tremendous cost—the painful death of God's own Son—and we Christians can easily forget how privileged we are.

As God's friends, we are invited to reverentially and respectfully enter His presence at any time. More than this, we are urged to do so, as God is actually eager to fellowship with us!

Abraham demonstrated the proper attitude toward this incredible blessing when he stood with God to speak as a man speaks to a friend—and then stepped even closer to speak to Him intimately. This attitude is both pleasing to God and profitable to His children.

God knows our doubts, but He rewards our faith.

Both Abraham and Sarah had doubts and misgivings about God's promise concerning an heir. Both of them responded in mocking laughter, and both of them attempted at one time to take matters into their own hands. But in the end, they believed God, and their faith was confirmed when Isaac was born.

Jacob had an imperfect understanding of the character of God, and his life was filled with cunning and trickery. Yet in the end he learned to rely on God's character, believing by faith that He would keep His promises—even when Jacob's common sense urged him to take matters into his own hands. God is looking for men and women of faith—men and women who will follow in the footsteps of those listed in Hebrews 11 and who are looking toward His Son, Jesus Christ. As we take small steps of faith, He is faithful to grow us more into the image of our Savior.

This world is not our home.

It is vital that Christians keep this truth in mind, for we are called to keep our eyes focused on eternity rather than on the world. But the world has a way of insinuating itself and its values into our thinking. Careers, academics, bills, obligations, even family will all demand our time and attention; this is a fact of life and cannot be entirely avoided while we live in the world. But we must also remember that we are *in* the world but not *of* the world—our home is in eternity.

This mind-set is one that must be renewed frequently, because the world around us will not give up the battle for our minds. We renew our minds by immersing ourselves in Scripture and by surrounding ourselves with other Christians who are like-minded. We reinforce the frame of mind by remembering, whenever we are tempted to worry or covet, that we are not going to be living on this planet forever.

We are citizens of a heavenly city, one that is not built by human hands and one that will last forever. Everything in this world—absolutely everything—will one day be destroyed by fire, and we must take care not to invest our lives into things that will be burned up.

⤳ Digging Deeper ⤳

1. What are some of the more important things you have learned from these studies?

2. Which of the concepts or principles have you found most encouraging? Which have been most challenging?

3. What aspects of "walking with God" are you already doing in your life? Which areas need strengthening?

4. Which of the characters that we've studied have you felt the most attracted to? How might you emulate that person in your own life?

✧ Taking It Personally ✧

5. Have you taken a definite stand for Jesus Christ? Have you accepted His free gift of salvation? If not, what is preventing you?

6. What areas of your personal life have been most convicted during this study? What exact things will you do to address these convictions? Be specific.

7. What have you learned about the character of God during this study? How has this insight affected your worship or prayer life?

8. List below the specific things you want to see God do in your life in the coming month. List also the things you intend to change in your own life during that time. Return to this list in one month, and hold yourself accountable to fulfill these things.

If you would like to continue in your study of Genesis, read the next title in this series: *Jacob and Egypt: The Sovereignty of God.*